Exiled

Exiled

The Last Days of Sam Houston

RON ROZELLE

Texas A&M University Press • College Station

First edition

This paper meets the requirements of ANSI/NISO Z39.48–1992 (Permanence of Paper).
Binding materials have been chosen for durability.
Manufactured in the United States of America

Library of Congress Cataloging-in-Publication Data

Names: Rozelle, Ron, 1952– author.
Title: Exiled : the last days of Sam Houston / Ron Rozelle.
Description: First edition. | College Station : Texas A&M University Press, [2017] | Includes bibliographical references and index.
Identifiers: LCCN 2017021369 | ISBN 9781623495862 (book/cloth : alk. paper) | ISBN 9781623495879 (ebook)
Subjects: LCSH: Houston, Sam, 1793–1863—Last years. | Houston, Sam, 1793–1863—Homes and haunts—Texas—Hunstville. | Governors—Texas—Biography. | Texas—History—1846–1950.
Classification: LCC F390.H84 R69 2017 | DDC 976.404092 [B]—dc23
LC record available at https://lccn.loc.gov/2017021369

For Zoë and Madeline,
two newly arrived granddaughters
to love Texas,

for Logan Kibodeaux,
who has loved her considerably longer,

and, as always,
for Karen

Old age hath yet his honor and his toil;

Death closes all: but something ere the end,

Some work of noble note, may yet be done,

Not unbecoming men that strove with gods.

—Tennyson, *Ulysses*

I would give no thought of what the world might say of me,

if I could only transmit to posterity the reputation

of an honest man.

—Sam Houston

Contents

A Note

In this attempt to present the story of Sam Houston and the events of the last dozen or so years of his remarkable life, every effort was made to locate and document facts and figures in sources both primary—particularly original documents and hundreds of Houstons' personal letters—and secondary, including numerous biographies and histories. At times suppositions are made in the narrative—based always on the established characteristics and beliefs of the subjects and the mores and realities of the era—to better relate the time and place, but no actual events were altered and no characters introduced who never existed.

The book is aimed at a general reading audience, not just an academic one, and it is hoped that both can find a story here worthy of its subject.

Prologue

Huntsville, Texas
May 1863

It was barely half a mile between his house and the prison, a short walk in former times and better days. And downhill most of the way. But he had turned seventy a couple of months before, and, given the stubborn aggravation of several decades-old war wounds and the natural decline caused by the decades themselves, what would have once been a pleasant stroll would prove a slow, painful trek. And the return trip would be uphill. So either Joshua or Jeff—slaves or servants, depending on if he had actually freed all his slaves in October of the previous year, as one popular yet unverified legend maintains—would have driven him in the buggy.

It's possible he got a few waves or the tips of a couple of hats along the way, from people on horses or in wagons or walking up the hill from town, under fragrant pines and cedars interspersed with oaks, sycamores, and pecans in full leaf by early May. But many folks would not have acknowledged him, especially if they had known what he was up to. And they *would* have known, because he had made this trip at least once by then and because Huntsville was a small town, where everybody pretty much knew everybody else's business.

He might have been wearing a blue velvet smoking cap he had lately taken a liking to instead of the wide-brimmed beaver hat he had long favored.[1] And instead of his ever-present walking stick, by now a crutch might have leaned against the seat.

Even though the chills of early spring had come and gone, he might still have draped a multihued Indian blanket over his shoulders, probably woven by either Cherokees or Coushattas. The first tribe had provided frequent sanctuary in his boyhood and early adulthood; the second, native to the Huntsville area and considerably friendlier than the belligerent, angry nations to the west and north, had recently sought and received his assistance when the Confederacy attempted to conscript Indians into its army.[2]

If not a native blanket, he might have worn a color-splashed cape or a light, festive shawl. For he did like to make an impression with his attire, having famously stood in the Senate and before assembled throngs in all manner of loud livery.

When he was helped down from the buggy on arrival, he would have steadied himself and looked up at the imposing fortress. Most people did. Though it had been there fifteen years—long enough for many generations of birds to have pecked out countless homesteads in the cracks and crannies in its high walls, making the big place a breathing, squawking thing—it was still enough of a commanding sight to get one's attention and hold it for a moment. Even now, more than a century and half on, its original walls long since sandwiched between red bricks, it is still impressive. And still a prison.

The construction of a state penitentiary was high on the itinerary of the first legislature elected in Texas after annexation as a state. A committee of three was tasked to select a site no larger than one hundred acres that would cost no more than five dollars each. Having agreed on the location, they paid $22 for the 4.8 acres where the prison itself would be built just up a slight hill from the town. Another 94 acres not too far away, thick with timber, was bought for $470.[3]

The legislation was specific in its requirements. The prison must be in a healthful climate and near a navigable body of water so that machinery, tools, and materials could be brought in and articles eventually made by the convicts sent out. Rehabilitation held no importance whatsoever in the agenda of that first legislature, but profit most certainly did. The Trinity River was close by, so those articles—whatever they turned out to be—could be floated down to Galveston's busy port.

The prison was to be surrounded by a secure wall made of "substantial materials" that would enclose a yard large enough for workshops to be constructed. For the convicts were to be kept busy performing whatever officials "deemed most profitable and useful to the state."[4] This meant that the only brick structure on the place—a small, one-story schoolhouse with chimneys at either end that had housed the Huntsville Academy—would have to eventually be razed or drastically repurposed.

Huntsville, a little village in the piney woods of northeastern Texas, was chosen from a shortlist of several possible sites for the prison. The fact that one of the members of the committee was from a nearby town had probably helped. But it was common knowledge that the strongest determining factor was that the old man standing beside the buggy lived in Huntsville.

Back in 1848, when the prison had been built, he hadn't yet fallen from grace.

• • •

Once inside, he paid his respects to Thomas Caruthers, the superintendent of the prison, before being escorted to the men he had come to see.[5] There weren't many of them, the surviving officers of the USS *Harriet Lane*, a federal side-wheel steamer captured five months earlier in the first hours of the first day of 1863 during what was already being called the Battle of Galveston. The enlisted crew had been quickly exchanged for Confederate prisoners and sent north, except for six black sailors who, though they were freemen in their home states, were deemed in Texas to be slaves in insurrection.[6]

The men had been taken prisoner by the Confederate forces under the command of General John B. Magruder, whom Robert E. Lee, in a reorganization of his general staff, had recently given the command of Texas, Arizona, and New Mexico. Magruder had vowed to wrench Galveston, the strategically important island and its bustling city and harbor, away from Union control and send the Yankees packing, which he had done; Galveston would remain in Confederate hands for the duration of the war.

The prisoners were first housed under armed guard in a cotton warehouse sixty miles north of the island in Houston City before being taken in wagons, in late April, another seventy miles up to Huntsville and the penitentiary.

They received their first visit within a day or two of their incarceration, the old man wanting to see firsthand that they were being treated with the respect and dignity prisoners of war should be afforded. He bristled when he learned that these men had been separated and put into cells with the thieves and murderers that generally ended up in the prison. It had taken only a curt word or two with Caruthers to get them segregated from the general population.

One story has it that he was instrumental in having some of them—certainly not the black men, who would have been confined in another section of the prison—granted short supervised visits into town to stretch their legs, which might not have actually happened. Already uneasy with

Yankees being in their midst at all, even locked up in what was already and would forever after be called the "Walls," the prospect of them roaming the roads and looking into windows wouldn't have sat well with Huntsville's citizens.

Prison officials weren't any too pleased about having them either, seeing the chance of an internal uprising—a feeble possibility at best, given their small number and the fact that they were probably happier playing checkers than planning a riot—or, worse yet, an attempt by federal forces to break them out, which might hinder the all-important manufacture of cotton cloth in the prison's textile mill, a major source of uniforms and tents for the Rebel army, producing something like a million and half yards per year.[7] It would also have provided a subsidy in Confederate script from President Jefferson Davis's war chest, though by then, nearly two years into the war, those coffers would have been significantly depleted.

There is no record of whether he was left alone with the men during their meetings or chaperoned by a guard. It wouldn't have mattered either way; he certainly had no current official secrets to share, nor probably did they. Neither is it known what they talked about. He would probably have listened to stories about their kinfolk in the North or told them tales of one or another of his famous exploits, for he was a gifted yarn spinner of great renown. They would have wanted news of the huge war that was raging, and he was a reliable source. He read whatever newspapers he could find and still corresponded with a few acquaintances in Texas and, to the extent that mail made it through the federal blockade, in Washington.

It is easy to imagine his looking at his pocket watch at the end and asking if they needed anything. Then he would have shaken their hands again and possibly said he hoped that all would be well soon and they could go home to their families. He might have handed them a bundle of sweet cakes (cookies) or a pie from home, baked not by his wife, whose Southern Belle upbringing had not included much in the way of cooking, but by the skeletal slave who had been her childhood playmate in Alabama and then sent along to Texas with her when she married.

And he might have mentioned the folly of this war that pitted parts of a still young, hard-won union against each other. He had been a persistent orator, over a stretch of several years, on that single topic from any stump he could climb up on and more famously on the Senate floor in league with giants like Daniel Webster and Henry Clay, both long in their graves. But the ringing words that had once stirred hearts and moved armies had finally fallen on deaf ears.

So he might have spent some of the last few of those words in a tiny room in a big prison on a spring day. By midsummer he would be dead.

The guards might have fumbled for how to address him as he walked slowly out to his buggy. He had been a general of the highest rank, twice the president of a republic, the governor of two states, a senator, congressman, official ambassador of and to the tribal nations, and a potentially viable candidate, more than once, for the office of president of the United States.

He was called many things in his time: hero, patriot, traitor, firebrand, maverick, Indian lover, genius, drunkard, and liberator. But history has chosen to simply call him Sam Houston. And that, by any measure, is sufficient.

• • •

Born in 1793 in the Shenandoah Valley of Virginia to a father who was a career soldier for whom his young son had little affection and a mother whom he adored, he was the fifth of nine children and definitely the most headstrong and free-spirited of the lot.

After Captain Houston's sudden death—not on a battlefield but in a tavern, reportedly of natural causes—when Sam was fourteen, Elizabeth Paxton Houston loaded up two big wagons with most of her possessions and all of her children and headed to a farm near Maryville, in eastern Tennessee, which her husband had purchased not long before his death.

Not fond of farming, young Sam was the constant recipient of lectures and threats from a pair of stern, no-nonsense older brothers whom he referred to as the "holy apostles."[8] He paid scant attention to them, or to obligations and responsibilities of any sort, a failing always forgiven by his lenient mother. Finally realizing that handing him a hoe or putting him behind a plow were wasted enterprises, the family decided to make him a clerk for one of his older brothers who ran a store in town.

Probably to the surprise of no one, keeping shelves filled and marking off lengths of calico didn't suit him any better than farming. So the willful youngster packed a few books from his late father's library, including Alexander Pope's translation of Homer and Charles Rollins's *Ancient History*, and ran away to live for a time with the Cherokees.

When his mother sent the brothers to fetch him home, he informed them, according to a family story handed down, that he "preferred measuring deer tracks to tape" and that he intended to stay put.[9] He suited his actions to his word for the next couple of years, during which time he learned the Indians' ways and customs and gained a profound respect for their values and worldview that would last him a lifetime. The Cherokee chief Oolooteka took a fatherly interest in him, giving him the Indian name Colonneh, which meant "Raven," the bird symbolic of, among other things, good fortune.[10] This chief would be the first of two extraordinary influences on Houston, each of them likely surrogates for the father who had had so little impact on him. Oolooteka's name meant "He Who Puts Away the Drum," meaning he saw peace as preferable to war, a philosophy that Houston would settle on years later.[11]

During this retreat from home and family Houston returned to Maryville occasionally just long enough to say hello to his mother and to purchase supplies, on credit. By the time he turned nineteen he had run up a considerable tab and had no means of settling it. His solution, surely the last one that anyone in his family would have predicted, was to open a school, even though he had never liked school and, in fact, had spent little time in one. Upon the family's arrival in Tennessee he had been promptly enrolled in Maryville Academy but rarely showed up for classes. "I often determined to lick him," the headmaster would remember much later when his delinquent charge had made a splash in the world, "but he would come up with such a pretty dish of excuses that I could not do it."[12]

He secured a "rickety cabin" outside town,[13] and he soon had twenty students registered, charging their families eight dollars per term, considered excessive at the time, payable one-third each in cash, corn, and homespun cotton cloth. His penchant for flashy outfits apparently started early, for he stipulated that the cloth must be in several colors.[14]

He kept the school open long enough to pay off his debt and in 1813 joined a group of other young men in taking their silver dollars from a drumhead, the customary ritual that delivered them into the Regular Army of the United States as privates. His older brothers saw it as a disgrace to the family that he would condescend to serve in that lowly rank when their father had been an officer. The young fellow with the silver dollar in his pocket—just over six feet tall, weighing 180 pounds, with unmanageable brown hair and enough of a Scotch-Irish glint in his eye to either charm or hinder—replied that though they did not know him then, "you shall hear of me."[15]

His mother, ever his champion regardless of his dubious path thus far, provided her written consent for him to go—he was not yet twenty-one—along with a musket and his late father's ring, engraved inside with a single word, "Honor," which he would wear for the rest of his life. Then, according to Houston's own account in his autobiography, she told him to "take this musket and never disgrace it, for remember, I had rather all my sons should fill one honorable grave than one of them should turn his back to save his life. . . . Remember, too, that while the door of my cabin is open to brave men, it is eternally shut against cowards."[16]

Overly fond of flowery language and often given to considerable embellishment, the older Houston might or might not have gotten the little speech exactly right. But given the fortitude and courage of his mother, most of his biographers have concurred that she would likely have said something very much like it.[17]

It took the young Houston not very long to be promoted to the rank of ensign, then in December 1813, to third lieutenant, the modern equivalent of a platoon commander. The following March he had become a bona fide hero at the age of twenty-one when he was seriously wounded, three times, at the Battle of Horseshoe Bend in present-day Alabama near the end of the War of 1812. His bravery and refusal of medical care when he could still be fighting caught the attention of General Andrew Jackson, who in time became yet another father figure, an association that proved to be life changing and, for the nation, history altering.

After the war, Houston, in the space of a single year, secured an appointment as an Indian agent; read enough law to pass the bar; hung out his shingle and opened a law office in Lebanon, Tennessee; and was appointed adjutant general of the state, which carried with it the rank of colonel.

In 1823 he won election to Congress as a Democrat, won reelection two years later, and in 1827, at the age of thirty-four, was elected governor of Tennessee, defeating a two-term incumbent. Two years later he married Eliza Allen, the eighteen-year-old daughter of a plantation owner. She left him less than four months later without explanation. In fact, little or no enlightenment regarding the cause of the separation would ever be forthcoming from either husband or wife.

The mystery has intrigued historians ever since. Some believe that one of his war injuries, in his groin, repulsed the young maiden. But the scenario given most credibility is that she was forced into the marriage with the governor by a family looking to elevate their social status, even though she already had a beau. Whatever the reason, Houston never criticized Eliza and let it be known that he would brook no criticism of her from anyone, standing ready to defend her honor at sword point if necessary. The marriage and its swift conclusion became, for him, a closed subject.

A week after her abrupt departure, Houston resigned the governorship in what he considered public disgrace and retreated, again, to the Cherokees, this time tumbling into sufficiently deep despair and drink to have his original moniker Raven often replaced with the less noble Oo-tse-tee-Ar-dee-tah-skee, which roughly translates as "Big Drunk."[18]

By 1829 he had sobered up enough to become a Cherokee citizen, to soldier on through a serious touch-and-go attack of malaria and, early the following year, to travel to Washington as the official representative of the tribe, presenting his credentials to the recently elected president, his mentor Andrew Jackson. Houston began writing a series of newspaper articles defending the inherent rights of Indians, and that summer he married Tiana Rogers, the daughter of a white man and an Indian woman, in a tribal ceremony.

In 1831, in the midst of his self-imposed exile, he made a quick trip to Tennessee after getting word that his mother was seriously ill in Maryville. He arrived in time to be at her bedside when she died in early September.[19]

In Washington the next year as an adviser, not an ambassador, with a Cherokee delegation, Houston soundly thrashed Ohio congressman William Stanbery one evening on Pennsylvania Avenue.[20] The congressman had made disparaging remarks about him on the floor of the House of Representatives, stopping just short of accusing him of fraudulent doings in a government contract with the Indian nations. Stanbery was avidly anti-Jackson politically, so it was somehow fitting that Houston employed a cane carved from a hickory limb from the Hermitage, the president's estate in Tennessee, to deliver the flogging.[21]

When Congress ordered Houston's arrest, he asked lawyer and sometimes poet Francis Scott Key, who in 1812 had penned the verses that would eventually become the lyrics to the national anthem, to defend him. The plea was self-defense (a pistol in Stanbery's possession apparently misfired during the walloping), but the House found Houston guilty by a vote of 106 to 89, finally choosing to merely reprimand him.

Dissatisfied with the light sentence, Stanbery introduced a resolution to bar Houston from the House of Representatives forever, which was quickly voted down by a huge majority. So he resorted to bringing criminal assault charges in the courts of the District of Columbia. The verdict of the hastily called proceeding was guilty, again, and Houston was fined five hundred dollars, which he would be allowed to pay out over several years.

Ironically, having been found guilty in not one but two trials ended up costing him no more than his attorney's fees, if there were any. The admonishment in the first case amounted to nothing more than a slap on the wrist, and his friend in the White House found the fine to be excessive in the second and issued a presidential pardon.[22] Even if he had not, by the time the first payment would have come due, Houston had traveled over a thousand miles to the Southwest and stepped headlong into his destiny.[23]

• • •

In the early 1830s American settlers in the northern Mexican state of Coahuila y Tejas who hadn't pulled up stakes and survived the longest and hardest journey of their lives to reside in a nation ruled by tyrants were becoming increasingly disgruntled with the autocratic stench drifting up from Mexico City.

Houston, already disgruntled after his various trials and tribulations, had for some time smelled a revolution brewing and perhaps heard a new life calling. Years later, when presented with a gift of some handsome Durhams on his way back east to serve in the Senate, he would say that he could "at long last do what he had originally gone to Texas to do—raise cattle."[24] Whether ranching is truly what most motivated him is arguable at best. But whatever the reason, he set his sights on Texas.

Late in 1832 he determined to make his way to northern Mexico and apply for "head rights"—one league, 4,428 acres, deeded to a qualifying head of a family (he and Eliza Allen were not yet legally divorced)—in the colony that the enterprising visionary Stephen F. Austin was quickly populating with pioneers migrating westward. Houston raised the necessary funds to make the journey and pay the mandatory fees, probably either from a loan or a gift outright from Andrew Jackson,[25] who continually proved to be a perpetual source of inspiration, guidance, financial support, and, it seems, the occasional whipping stick.

Historians have made much of the notion of Jackson having pushed Houston toward Texas. Whatever the extent of his participation, at the very least the president, who could read a map and perhaps even see into the future, would have seen his protégé, who was totally dedicated to the Union, settling into that hotbed of unrest as potentially good for any expansion opportunities that might present themselves.

Houston's Indian wife, Tiana, chose not to join him on the adventure.[26] She had put up with the worst of his drinking and tantrums during his span of melancholia and despair and nursed him back to health during his bout of malaria, and she probably figured she had done her bit and that no further sacrifices were called for.

So in December 1832 Sam Houston went to Texas alone. Biographers disagree on just how he made the fateful crossing of his personal Rubicon at the border of the United States and its territories. Marshall De Bruhl maintains that it would not have been atop the galloping, splashing steed that legend recounts and both Marquis James and James Haley report, but via the major crossing at that location, a ferry paddled across the muddy Red River just south of present-day Fort Towson, Oklahoma.[27] However he negotiated the river, he rode into the vast region that would very soon become synonymous with his own name.

Later that month his request for head rights was approved once he joined the Roman Catholic Church, for reasons purely practical rather than spiritual since only Catholics could own land in Mexico.[28] He wasted little time before jumping into the growing disagreement between the newly arrived settlers, who styled themselves "Texians," and the ever-fluctuating government of Mexico, which had tossed out its democratic Constitution of 1824 and replaced it with totalitarian rule headed by alternating dictators who seemed, via various coups, to be taking turns.

After opening a law office in Nacogdoches—perhaps because it was the first town of any significance he came to—Houston began writing to President Jackson on occasion, describing the beauty of this land and calling attention to how appealing it might be to the neighboring nation that was currently spreading its wings. Literally spreading them, in fact, on a popular map of the United States published that year on which cartographer Joseph Churchman cleverly superimposed a gigantic American eagle, its head over New England resolutely facing the Atlantic Ocean and Europe, proudly protruding breast and torso over the bulk of the existing states, legs and talons dropping down over Florida, tail feathers over the Arkansas Territory, and its mighty wings sweeping back over the vast midwestern unorganized territory to the border of the Oregon Country currently in dispute between America and Great Britain. The map was a perfect visual representation of the growing notion of divine entitlement sweeping the country, which, a decade later, newspaper editor John L. O'Sullivan would coin as "Manifest Destiny."[29]

In Texas the settlers probably couldn't have cared less about the expansion of the United States; they just wanted better treatment from Mexico or, better yet, to be left alone. But Sam Houston, who was elected as a delegate from Nacogdoches to the 1832 convention seeking separation from the state of Coahuila and statehood for Texas in the Mexican confederation, surely saw early on both goals as finally dovetailing into one. He would go on to prove, more than once, that he was perfectly capable of juggling two or more grand designs at the same time.

Over the next three years he made several trips to Washington and New York, usually on business for his legal client the Galveston Bay and Texas Land Company, and quickly marched up the ranks of leadership in the Nacogdoches militia.

In November 1835, while armed conflicts were flaring up between Texian militia and Mexican troops, a group of representatives from most areas of Texas convened in San Felipe to hammer out a course of action. They called the meeting a "consultation," believing designating it the more threatening "convention" might send the message to Mexico, a volatile nation well acquainted with revolutions, that another one was imminent. During the meeting a slate of officials was elected for a provisional government. Land grant entrepreneur Stephen F. Austin, favoring diplomacy over bloodshed, was defeated for governor by Henry Smith, a settler from Tennessee who was hell-bent for war. A regular army was established, with two-year enlistments and US Army regulations, to serve alongside numerous groups of volunteers with their own officers and few, if any, rules at all. Houston was unanimously elected to serve as the standing army's commander, with the rank of major general.[30]

Five months later, on the second day of March 1836—his forty-third birthday—Houston, along with fifty-nine other men assembled at Washington-on-the-Brazos while the Alamo was under siege at San Antonio de Bexar, voted to declare Texas independent of Mexico. The declaration had been written literally overnight (borrowing liberally from another document produced in Philadelphia sixty years previously) and was officially signed the next day.[31]

Practically before the ink was dry on the parchment Houston was named the general of the Army of the Republic of Texas—such as it was, comprising mostly volunteers who saw orders as suggestions and military precision and demeanor as pure folly.[32]

The ensuing revolution spun itself out as dramatically and swiftly as one of the tornados that sometimes dropped down and roared across that part of the world. With the exception of the thirteen-day siege of the Alamo, its skirmishes and battles were brief affairs.[33] George Collinsworth's capture of Goliad took a mere matter of minutes, as did James Bowie's, James Fannin's, and Ben Milam's defeat of General Martín Perfecto de Cos in San Antonio. The Runaway Scrape, Mexican general Antonio Lopez de Santa Anna's pursuit of Houston's troops after the fall of the Alamo, thundered its way toward San Jacinto like a frantic footrace between giants. It took Houston's motley army less than twenty minutes to defeat the much larger, better-trained force and win the battle and the war.

Of the major Texan heroes of the revolution, only Houston would survive it. Ben Milam was killed in December 1835 during the Bexar siege; William Barrett Travis, Davy Crockett, and James Bowie fell in the Alamo; James Fannin fell in the battle at Goliad; and Stephen Austin died of pneumonia in December 1836. "I stand the last almost," Houston would famously say years later, "of a race."[34]

Of that little fraternity whose names were given to towns, cities, counties, and innumerable streets and avenues, he alone would be granted a long life in which to render further service to Texas, initially as the republic's first and third president and then, after Texas gained statehood, as one of its first senators in Washington and later its seventh governor.

Though Stephen F. Austin is commonly referred to as the "Father of Texas," it was Houston—who by most accounts first bestowed the title on Austin—who commanded the army that won Texas' independence, headed its first government, and practically hand-delivered it into the Union as the twenty-eighth state.

By that spring day in 1863 when he rode down the hill to the prison in Huntsville to visit the captured officers of the *Harriet Lane*, he had been known for almost thirty years as the "Hero of San Jacinto." But current events had convinced most of the people who had conferred that honorific that San Jacinto lay in the remote and misty past. A bigger conflict filled up their present world.

And in this one, they figured, old Sam had lined up on the wrong side.

Part One

1850

If I could only get you to love this place as I do,

I would be perfectly satisfied.

One

One of the first things Margaret Lea Houston did on the first day of January in 1850 was dip the narrow nib of her pen into a little ink pot and begin a letter to her husband. It was a common ritual for her, conducted almost daily during his long and frequent absences. Half a continent away, in Washington, DC, Senator Sam Houston was equally diligent, sometimes sending three or more long missives—scratched out on crisp stationery, sometimes at his desk while a bloviating fellow senator rambled on but usually late at night in his rented room after long days at the Capitol—in a single mail pouch back to Texas.

"Another year has commenced," Margaret wrote on that frigid January morning, her perfectly straight, delicate characters like the footprints of tiny birds in snow. "May it be the last, that shall find us this far apart."[1] It would not be.

"Your little ones were up before dawn this morning," she wrote, referring to Sam Jr., aged seven; Nannie, four; and Maggie, who "though only [in] her second new year, danced and chirped more merrily than usual." Another girl, Mary William—later truncated to Mary Willie—would arrive a few months later. The others, three boys and another girl, would follow in due course over the next dozen years.

Margaret moved on to other things in her letter, providing a brief report of a rousing Sons of Temperance meeting in town and news of her sister's and brother's families and the possibility of their soon paying visits to Huntsville "owing to the conditions of the roads." And there was this: "I am more attracted to our home and neighbors than ever. If I could only get you to love this place as I do, I would be perfectly satisfied."[2]

In fact, the senator was already sufficiently enamored of their "rude cabin," as Margaret sometimes called it, to profess being homesick for it in several of the many letters that traveled from Washington to Huntsville. But his young wife's frequent weighing of her own contentment regarding hearth and home against what she obviously perceived as the lacking of it on his part is reflective of larger concerns that had been ongoing since the beginning of their marriage and would continue until shortly before the end of it.

When Margaret was a newlywed just out of her teens, she had quietly established her private battle lines on three fronts: to wean her famously tippling husband off demon liquor (so opposed was she to its sinful allure that she had refused to take even a small dram of whiskey as a sedative in 1847 when she had a tumor sliced out of her breast);[3] to see him immersed—spiritually and physically—in the Baptist Church; and to pull him away from his public life and back to his family.

By now, in the tenth year of their marriage, she had achieved an apparent victory in the first battle but still held out hope and sent up prayers for the second and third. While he had steadfastly refused to be baptized and had given some lip service but thus far provided no actual evidence of stepping back out of politics, Houston *had* stopped drinking, apparently in earnest and for good.

There had been just one rather melodramatic backslide, in the early 1840s during his second term as president of the Republic of Texas. Margaret, having a difficult time with her second pregnancy—she had miscarried the previous year—had been persuaded by her mother, a short, wide, domineering widow to whom the employment of forceful persuasion came naturally, to travel with her for a prolonged stay at Margaret's younger sister Antoinette's home some hundred miles away at Grand Cane, near the curving Trinity River just north of the town of Liberty.

The Houstons were living at the time at Washington-on-the-Brazos, where Houston had ordered the capital be relocated when Mexican troops moved dangerously close to San Antonio, which was too close to Austin for his comfort. The declaration that ignited the revolution was signed in Washington; over the next five years the various seats of government hopped around to several locations, nudged always by the movements of the Mexican army.

In all likelihood Houston probably welcomed this move, since he had been unhappy with the decision of his predecessor to pack up the government and move it to the tiny town named after Stephen F. Austin from a much larger one named after—no surprise here—himself.

While the Texas Congress settled into a small wooden building that wasn't quite large enough to accommodate it, President and Mrs. Houston were the houseguests of a family named Lockhart until more suitable accommodations could be made for the first family. During his hosts' absence one afternoon during Margaret's stay at her sister's, Houston decided to read for a while on the four-poster bed in his bedroom.

Unfortunately, he also decided to fondle and consider a jug of Madeira presented to him that day as a gift intended for Eliza Lockhart. A combination of his loneliness for Margaret, a long-deprived preference for Madeira in particular, and the fact that his alcohol-craving system had had to make do for a few years with orange peels muddled into simple bitters caused him to, over the course of a long afternoon, polish off the entire contents. Sometime that night, when the wine had time to run its course and have its effect, he sat staring at one of the looming bedposts long enough to take exception to its stoic arrogance. He stumbled out to a nearby outbuilding and awakened Frank, his slave, instructing him to find an ax and chop the thing down.

Whatever he thought of it, Frank must have first concluded that Houston was his master and his president, and he set about carrying out his assigned task with vigor. Awakened by the commotion and fearing an assassination attempt, the Lockharts burst through the bedroom door just as the heavy post hit the floor.[4]

When he was coherent enough to make amends, Houston had his horse saddled and brought up. There's no record of what explanation or compensation he made to the Lockharts, but in regard to Margaret, there was nothing to do but get himself to her as quickly as possible, relate the sordid tale, and beg her forgiveness.[5] She promptly gave it, perhaps seeing the episode as something of a blessing, tightening the shackles even stronger on a moral weakness she could never condone.

Years later, on that New Year's morning in 1850, Margaret, amid her bustling children and beside a good fire in the grate, wrote, toward the end of the pages that would soon make their slow trek to Washington, DC, "I shall be looking for one of your long letters, and tell me dearest when may I look for *you.* I will not suffer myself to think for a moment of your staying till the close of the session; for I do not think I can possibly be reconciled to it."[6]

As it turned out, she wouldn't have to be. For a little over a month later, in mid-February, Houston made a hasty trip to Huntsville, or as hasty as stagecoaches and riverboats could transport him across fourteen hundred miles of wilderness dotted only sporadically with clusters of civilization, and then back again.

That journey—long and arduous, involving full days in bouncing coaches, uncomfortable nights in way-station inns, and constant delays en route due to temperamental weather, swollen rivers, and impassable roadways—can easily be seen, in retrospect, as having been completely avoidable. It was only a few months until the summer recess, and, more important, it was a pivotal time when national events and impending legislation made it imperative that every senator be in attendance. The current debate over a complex compromise bill that might break the deadlock between the northern and southern states, thus preventing a severance of the two, had reached a fever pitch. And Sam Houston of Texas was a particularly vocal participant.

But it was obvious to him that Margaret needed him at home. Such was the influence of the woman who, at twenty, had stepped into his world when he was forty-six, after two marriages and enough of a life already lived to stand complete for most men, and captivated him entirely.

She was his muse, his soul mate, and his confidante. And neither of them could have had an inkling, in early 1850, of how much he would need her beside him for what lay in their future. Like Odysseus, whose heroic exploits he had read about in one of his father's books on his boyhood adventures with the Cherokees back in Tennessee, he would one day be old, home from his wars, and facing the greatest battle of all. Without his own Penelope to support him, he would likely not be up to the task.

Two

Margaret sometimes told the story, to her children and her close friends, of the first time she saw him, which was a month and a few days after her seventeenth birthday, on a school trip to New Orleans in May 1836. The minister and his wife who ran the Pleasant Valley Academy, near Marion, Alabama, had maneuvered their group of young ladies as close to the banks of the Mississippi River as possible in the bustling throng of several thousand waiting to witness the arrival of the famous liberator of Texas who was currently all the rage. This was especially so among wide-eyed southern girls of some advantage in society, well versed in Sir Walter Scott's romantic novels and Sir Thomas Mallory's *Le Morte d'Arthur* and much in awe of heroes.[1]

Finally, the ship appeared downriver, delivering Houston to New Orleans from Galveston so a surgeon could attempt repairs on an ankle that a Mexican musket ball had shattered a month before during the Battle of San Jacinto. The little vessel everybody waved at out on the wide expanse of swift-moving water, the schooner *Flora*, was a shabby affair much in need of some new lumber, fresh paint, and sails in better repair. Currently under tow behind a steamboat and listing badly, it must have seemed an awfully disappointing conveyance for so grand an arrival.

The fact was Houston couldn't afford a better transport. A Texas Navy ship, the *Liberty*, had sailed to New Orleans at the same time for repairs, but he was denied passage on the ship by the interim president of Texas, David G. Burnet, who disliked—and was equally disliked by—his commanding general.[2] So Houston secured a berth on the *Flora* with a personal IOU written out to the captain.[3] When the sad craft was tied off at the dock, so many people scampered over the gangplank that it tilted precariously toward the shore, causing the captain to yell out that the boat was in danger of sinking.

Order was finally restored amid much cheering and hoopla, and finally—according to the recollection, many years later, of someone in the crowd—Houston, ashen and weak, waited for quiet and delivered a brief address that began with him expressing his need, despite his physicians' advice that he should not speak, to thank everyone for their "sympathy for Texas." Then, according to that fellow who claimed to have promptly jotted down what he remembered of the talk immediately after its conclusion, the frail speaker said that, though Texas had "conquered Santa Anna and his bloody soldiers . . . she has another grander victory to gain before she is really free and great; she must conquer herself, her passions, and her sins. And in the second battle we need large recruits of pious women and ministers of the gospel."[4]

Either the voyage on the wobbly ship or delivering the short speech, perhaps a combination of both, must have drained him of what little energy he had left, for according to several accounts he collapsed while leaving the *Flora*. As he was carried to a waiting buggy and taken unconscious to the hospital for his surgery and subsequent recovery, the crowd cheered loudly and a band played what the scribbling recorder called "rousing airs."[5]

Even if the witness correctly transcribed the talk and if young Margaret was close enough to hear it, it is highly unlikely that she envisioned herself, that day, as one of the pious women or gospel ministers that he requested. It would be two years before she would give herself over completely to a religious faith so strong that it would be her unwavering anchor for the rest of her days. And she never claimed to have dreamed or predicted, at seventeen, that she would eventually marry Sam Houston. But she did tell a friend that she had a strong premonition that she would meet him one day.[6]

Three years later, she was proven right.

In May 1839 Houston, having recently completed his term as the first president of the Republic of Texas, was in Mobile, Alabama, on his way to a visit with Andrew Jackson, two years out of the White House and retired to the Hermitage, his home near Nashville, Tennessee. Seeking potential investors in a company he was involved in—a coastal Texas town site east of Galveston at Sabine Pass—Houston met a fellow named Martin Lea, a prominent citizen of Mobile. The two apparently hit it off, and Lea accompanied his new friend to several social functions where local citizens with deep pockets would be thick on the ground.[7]

One such gathering, a garden party being given by Lea's younger sister Antoinette and her husband, William Bledsoe, at their home, Spring Hill, was a church social in honor of Antoinette's and Martin's mother, a widow who had recently sold the family plantation and had some cash needing investing that could conceivably find its way into Texas.[8]

After making his spiel to Nancy Lea, Houston spent a while that late afternoon in the garden doing what several political campaigns had made him quite adept at: mingling and laying on the charm. Mistaking an attractive girl with violet eyes and wavy brunette hair as his hostess Antoinette,[9] he is said to have remarked to someone that "if she were not already married, I believe I would give that charming young lady a chance to say 'no.'"[10] Having either heard it or heard about it, Antoinette pulled her introverted older sister—maybe recalling her premonition of three years before—out of a conversation and over to the guest that was the object of everyone's attention.

And there, amid dishes of fresh strawberries and cream and platters of teacakes on tables set out under magnolia trees, with probably bowls of lemonade and punch but certainly not a mint julep or bourbon toddy to be had—the Leas were all Baptist to the core Margaret Lea of Marion, Alabama, barely twenty years old and on summer recess from the Judson Institute, a college founded only the year before by her home church, was formally introduced to Sam Houston of Texas who, at forty-six, was twenty-six years her senior.

Soon after, they strolled through the garden together, and he picked a carnation that she placed in her hair. A bit later, he pointed to a particularly bright star in the night sky and asked if she thought it might be their star of destiny.[11]

Before he left for Tennessee, what Nancy Lea thought was a series of visits from Houston for the purpose of providing maps for her to ponder and answers to her questions regarding the Sabine Pass town site was actually the surreptitious courtship of her daughter being conducted right under her nose. When she figured it out, the plump, raven-haired matriarch of the Leas calculated the plusses and minuses of the new development.

As a businesswoman she was inclined to be in favor of not only investing in the Texas land speculation possibilities Houston represented but was considering actually moving there. And in the eyes of the old, deep-rooted families of Dixie, the marriage of her daughter to a national figure who had been a victorious general, the governor of a state, and the president of a republic might move her family up a rung or two on the ever-important social ladder.

But as a mother, she had to consider carefully the flip side of this perhaps deceptively shiny coin. Houston was barely a dozen years younger than herself and over twice that much older than Margaret and was notorious for his drinking, swearing, and quick temper. He had, after all, violently pummeled a man in a Washington street with a cane.

Another serious concern for this widow of a Baptist preacher and herself a pillar of the Siloam Baptist Church in Marion was that Houston had been married and divorced:[12] twice, actually, if any official credence was given to his Indian tribal ceremony with Tiana Rogers. He was also, because of the Mexican law regarding the ownership of land, technically a Roman Catholic, which might, had Margaret Lea known about it at the time, have been his most egregious flaw. For her, being a papist probably trumped being a divorcé. Also, though he would invoke God's blessing on this or that matter in speeches when it was to his advantage to do so, Sam Houston wasn't much of a churchgoer unless there were voters to woo there.

In the matter of a romance with young Margaret Lea, the cards were heavily stacked against him on her mother's table. But in Margaret's eyes, it appears to have been nothing less than a case of love at first sight. And the numerous speculations as to the reason for it proffered over the next century and a half—the frontrunners being her psychological need for a replacement for her beloved father who died when she was fifteen, her infatuation with a very real hero after having read about so many fictional ones, and (the least likely, given her beauty and social standing) a determination to marry practically anyone who asked—all lose much or all of their steam when juxtaposed with how the rest of her life would be spent and to whom she would be completely devoted and wanted beside her constantly not only in this life but, the constant focus of her hopes and prayers, in the next.

After Houston left to sell more scripts for the Texas venture and to visit Jackson, Margaret waited patiently for the letters he had promised to write. When one finally arrived from Nashville (no copies of his letter survive), she responded on the seventeenth of July, the first of many hundreds between them that their great-great-granddaughter would spend a decade cataloguing and editing late in the twentieth century. Margaret worked her thoughts through a complete first draft before carefully penning the one she posted.[13]

"At last," she wrote, "I have heard from you and the tidings are truly welcome I assure you. My answer may be taken as a strong evidence of that, for it is the first I have addressed to any gentleman." She went on, in a precise and delicate hand, to describe Marion, the Alabama town to which she had by then returned, "surrounded by its green hills, groves, and bowers, it is like a sweet wood-nymph untarnished by the wiles and cold deception of the world."[14]

Though her mother might at the time have read something ominous into the wily and cold deception bit, Margaret had a different intention. In the next paragraph she said she was among "her childhood friends," referring to the books by her favorite authors in the library of her brother's house, where she and her mother were staying. And though she professed to be happy to be there, she allowed there were "those absent whose station within my heart remains unfilled."[15]

She could, of course, have been talking about friends or loved ones who had moved away or died, like her father, or even books from the library that had been lost or loaned out and not returned. But Sam Houston—ever in possession of a healthy, headstrong ego—could have only seen one possibility when he read it. "I am in the library" she continued. "How solemn the place! Sacred to holy musings and communion with the genius of ages gone bye [*sic*]! I am in the midst of a band of heroes, both ideal and real, and sages with their wisdom are here and yet though it may seem sacrilegious, my heart is not with them today." Then, the reason for her distraction: "Last night I gazed long upon our beauteous emblem the star of my destiny," Margaret wrote, referring to the star Houston had pointed out that first evening, "and my thoughts took the form of verse, but I will not inscribe them here, for then you might call me a romantic star-struck young lady."[16]

The poem she alluded to was written in the sentimental, sometimes forcibly rhymed, poetic style of the day, similar to that of her contemporary fellow southerner Edgar Allan Poe. Six carefully measured quatrains in length, it was an ode addressed to the flower Houston had picked for her in her sister's garden. In the third stanza she addresses the carnation:

He placed thee in my hand, that friend
Who now doth distant roam.
I took thee—little thinking then
How dear thou wouldst become.

. . . .

Time onward flies and swift advance
The years when friends are few,
The years when I shall live perchance
Like thee to whither too.

Thou sweet memento! Gentle flower!
Say will he cherish me,
And love me in that dark hour
As now I cherish thee?[17]

Margaret titled the poem "Lines to a Withered Pink"—carnations were commonly called pinks in that time and place—and she wouldn't show it to Houston until two years later, on the first anniversary of their marriage.

In Tennessee, after a week of imbibing and reminiscing with Jackson, Houston moved on to Maryville, his boyhood home, to visit family still living there. Then he stopped over in Alabama on his way back to Texas and checked into the Eagle Hotel, across the street from the Lea house.[18] During his visit he fell ill with a cold or the flu. Nancy Lea, in an obvious attempt to cleanse his soul and rid him of his sordid past, read scriptures to him, or rather over him, as he lay a feverish, captive audience.

When her heretofore submissive daughter had dug in her dainty heels and stated her intention, apparently even before Houston had stated his, her mother had accepted the inevitable and determined to make the best of it. Recovered from his illness and his exorcism Houston proposed, Margaret accepted, and her mother began making arrangements to close out her affairs in Alabama and move to Texas. The marriage would take place on some future date, allowing sufficient time to pass for an appropriate period of engagement.

In June, before exchanging love notes with Margaret, Houston had itemized in a letter to an old friend in Tennessee a list of "five things on earth" that he loved: "a fine woman, a fine horse, a fine dog, a Game Cock, and fine arms."[19] However his ledger stood on the last four things, in the summer of 1839 he seemed very much in possession of the first.

• • •

By late summer he was back in Nacogdoches, fuming about Mirabeau B. Lamar, a native of Georgia who had served gallantly at San Jacinto and was now Houston's successor as president. That they had both fought against Santa Anna's Mexican army in the revolution was perhaps the only common denominator between these two, and their views on governing set them worlds apart. And on a purely personal level, they just did not like each other.

Lamar saw Houston as reckless, egotistical, and overbearing, once calling him "a bloated mass of iniquity." When a book was published in 1846 titled *Sam Houston and His Republic*, Lamar wrote to his friend and fellow Houston enemy David Burnet, "His republic! That is true; for the country literally belongs to him and the people [are] his slaves. I can regard Texas as very little more than Big Drunk's big ranch."[20] He also considered Houston's almost total absence of formal education as a deficit for a leader and for a civilized gentleman. Lamar, who saw himself as a Renaissance man—in his youth he had excelled at both fencing and oil painting—would come to be called the "Father of Texas Education," striving during his administration to establish public schools by granting land and funds, putting the republic in dire straits financially.

Houston saw Lamar as not much more than a dandified writer of poetry; apparently it was fine with Houston if his twenty-year-old Southern Belle fiancée translated her innermost thoughts into verse, but for a grown man to do so was another matter entirely. He also took exception to how he dressed, which was very much in the French fashion; Lamar's middle name was Bonaparte, which must have greatly amused Houston.

One of the things Lamar did when elected to succeed Houston was toss out the flag of the republic that Houston had approved as president: a bright gold star on a field of deep blue. Lamar replaced it with a white star set amid a red, white, and blue tricolor.[21] Plopping his star, bland and colorless, down on a rehashed French flag didn't, of course, sit well with Houston.[22]

But what put the two most at odds was where they stood on the treatment of Indians. Houston's views were well known. His close association with the Cherokees and his deep reverence for their traditions went all the way back to his boyhood, and he had later been that tribe's official ambassador to the United States. His work on behalf of peoples native to the lands they had lived on for centuries was the only source of serious disagreement between Houston and his mentor, Andrew Jackson.[23] Though in 1813 Jackson had sent a young Creek boy orphaned in the Battle of Horseshoe Bend home to his childless wife, Rachel, and raised him in their household,[24] he essentially considered Indians as an inconvenient impediment to national expansion. Lamar agreed with Jackson, but to a further extreme. He was an avowed hater of all Indians, and as the newly elected president of Texas, he had made it one of his highest goals to either drive the Cherokee and the Comanche tribes from the republic or eradicate them.[25]

Houston was livid, to put it mildly, at how the republic he had fought for was being run, putting his contempt into forceful words in a speech in Nacogdoches, specifically denouncing the Lamar campaign against Indians.[26] Then, possibly not bothering to run the idea past Margaret back in Alabama, he announced his candidacy for Congress, meeting now in the newly chosen capital of Texas, it having been relocated from the already bustling Houston City on Buffalo Bayou north of Galveston to a little hamlet called Waterloo, more than 150 miles away on the north bank of the Colorado River.[27] Stephen F. Austin had died in 1836, and the place was renamed in honor of the late "Father of Texas," which was probably just as well. It might have been construed as a dark omen, given fairly recent events in world history, for a president named Bonaparte to govern in a town named Waterloo.

It wasn't unprecedented for a former president to serve as a congressman. John Quincy Adams was currently doing it, though Houston would hardly have appreciated the comparison to a man he detested. Once elected, Houston moved to Austin, declaring it, on first sight, "the most unfortunate site upon earth for the seat of government."[28]

• • •

The date for the wedding was originally set for February but had to be postponed at least twice due to pressing legislative business in Texas, where President Lamar was spending too much money and killing too many Indians for Congressman Houston's taste. Then in early spring, hoping to avoid a ceremony filled with Leas and lemonade in Alabama, Houston stood anxiously on the dock in Galveston awaiting the ship carrying the Bledsoes, Nancy Lea, and, he assumed, Margaret for a business trip having to do with the Sabine town site. When it became apparent that

Margaret was not with them, Nancy Lea had quickly taken the wheels off any scheme he might have had for the marriage to take place in Texas. "My dear General," she said, according to a much-repeated family story, "my daughter is in Alabama. She goes forth in the world to marry no man. The one who receives her hand will receive it in my home and nowhere else."[29]

Finally, on May 9, 1840, almost exactly one year after their first meeting, a roomful of guests was assembled in the home of Henry and Serena Lea in Marion. A small group of musicians was ready to begin playing, and Margaret, waiting in another room, was resplendent in the wedding dress she had made herself of white satin, purple silk, and blue muslin, having "not gone to any expense," she had written her mother, "which I thought you would object to."[30]

At the last moment Henry took Houston aside and, as the surrogate for Margaret's and his deceased father, nervously told him the family would appreciate it if he would explain the reason for his failed first marriage to Eliza Allen before this one could take place. Houston surely pondered, in the span of complete silence that followed, the moral dilemma he suddenly found himself in, weighing his love for Margaret and the heartbreak he might now cause her against an honorable vow he had kept for years. Finally, he told Henry that if they expected him to break it now, they would have to "pay the fiddler" and call everything off.[31]

Margaret's mother settled the issue, as succinctly as she settled most of her business. She waved her stubby hand for the proceedings to commence and cast her lot, and her daughter's, on whatever fate had in store for them.

• • •

A decade later, in early 1850, several of those in attendance that day were settled in Texas, which had by then made the transition from republic to statehood. Antoinette and William Bledsoe lived near the Trinity River in Grand Cane, and Sam and Margaret had settled in Huntsville with their three small children, though the senator was away at the national capital much of the time. Nancy Lea moved from place to place, staying sometimes for months on end in the home of one offspring or another in Texas and Alabama, not so much as a guest but as more of a commanding matriarch who raised her banner for a time in her currently designated flagship.

In a letter dated January 2, 1850, Sam Houston encouraged Margaret to have portraits painted of the children by George R. Allen, a well-known artist who would soon be in Huntsville. He also told her to "by no means fail" to have her mother's done as well. He saw a keen resemblance between their youngest, Maggie, and his mother-in-law, and he wished for Maggie to have the picture one day to remember her by.[32] Margaret, ever thriftier than her free-spending husband, nixed the idea of paintings of the children. But one was done of her mother.

It's a somber study. Her resolute features—lips clinched shut, eyelids lowered to something hovering between deep contemplation and a warning—are framed by a snugly tied bonnet. Her black dress is nearly indistinguishable from the dark backdrop, and the only light seems to be radiating from that ominous visage, as if some great, terrible truth resided there. Perhaps the most telling detail is at the very bottom of the canvas, where she is holding an open Bible in one plump hand while pressing emphatically down on a page with the tip of the index finger of the other, indicating surely what she knew to be the one true source of the only answer to any conceivable question and the solution to any worldly dilemma. Whether Maggie, who lived until 1906, ended up with the painting or if she ever saw a resemblance between its stoic subject and herself is unknown. It now hangs in the Heritage Society at Sam Houston Park in Houston.

But at the beginning of 1850 Nancy Lea was very much alive, Maggie was not yet two, Senator Houston was half a continent away, and Margaret was in trouble. She knew well enough from the steady stream of his letters that her husband was currently embroiled in the debate over a proposed compromise bill, a matter of supreme national importance and one of particular significance to Texas, since one of the primary provisions being debated included reshaping the state's boundaries. Margaret knew that Houston needed to be about important business in Washington. But she also knew that, as essential as his work there was, she needed for him to come home.

Three

When Sam Houston and Thomas Jefferson Rusk, who served as secretary of war in the interim government during the war with Mexico, were sent to Washington as the first senators from the newly annexed state of Texas in 1846, the Union, having just turned seventy, was experiencing a serious case of growing pains.

The Europeans who had settled the upper region of the eastern seaboard two centuries before—most of them Puritans in quest of a strict, insular utopia—had found a cold and inhospitable land that pretty much matched their austere disposition: some of it rolling hills that would make fine farms but some not suitable for much more husbandry than rocky vegetable gardens and rugged fruit and nut trees. Their neighbors to the south, mostly Cavaliers—King's Men—who had been defeated by the Puritans in England's long, bloody war between monarch and parliament, had found an immense agrarian paradise with abundantly rich, fertile soil and temperate seasons. From the beginning, New England's future was destined to be primarily industry. The lower colonies' would be agriculture.

The first rumblings of discontent between the inhabitants of the two regions arose when they organized themselves into a disparate collection of bickering, independent colonies clinging nervously to the eastern edge of the immense continent that sprawled out behind them, unexplored and most of it unclaimed (except, of course, by the resourceful societies of natives who had resided there from time immemorial).

Their past histories in the old world and their differing interests and plans in the new one created, between North and South, a metaphorical Hadrian's Wall that would only grow taller and thicker as time progressed. President Jefferson's purchase of the Louisiana Territory in 1803 inflated the United States by some eight hundred thousand square miles, making it both apparent and providential to southerners and northerners alike that new states should eventually fill up all that land like so many patches sewn onto a gigantic quilt.

Then the birth of the Republic of Texas, after Houston's army's stunning victory at San Jacinto, changed not only the balance of power and influence in what would come to be known as the American Southwest but its character as well. The old romantic shades of Spain and Mexico gave way to the hardy, brash bravado of intrepid pioneers descendant from a hodgepodge of nations. A handful of years later, when Texas became a state—again primarily because of Houston—the Union broadened both its boundaries and its outlook, taking a giant step farther westward with the admission of the big, bold, proud, and sometimes arrogant land that perfectly reflected the temperament of its most famous founding father.

By March 1846, when Sam Houston, outfitted in uncharacteristically conservative, formal garb—except for a vibrant spotted vest made from the pelt of a Mexican jaguar[1]—took the senatorial oath with such luminaries as Clay, Webster, John C. Calhoun, and Martin Van Buren, the cause for division between North and South, having run its long course through boundary disputes, differing currencies, and sundry other squabbles, had been rendered down to essentially one sticking point: chattel human slavery. More specifically, to the heated debate regarding whether western territories seeking statehood should enter the union as free or slave states.

Essentially, the northern states planted their puritanical feet in the moral high ground of abolitionism, and threats of secession were quickly becoming the coins of the realm in the South. The sowing and reaping that provided the economic infrastructure in Dixie depended heavily on the ownership of slaves, which was not the case in the North, where a steady influx of desperate European immigrants could be hired for practically nothing to work long days in industry.

In fact, when confronted with the moral indignation of northerners regarding slavery, southerners often maintained that in most cases their slaves were treated better than impoverished, grossly underpaid Irish workers in northern factories. But this argument ran only so far since one group, whatever the harsh realities of their lives, were free and the other, however kindly they might have been treated, were not.

Since his arrival Houston had found himself consistently at odds with other senators of both his party and geographical region, not on the issue of slavery, which he defended as an absolute economic necessity in the South, but as a vocal champion of Indian rights and a steadfast defender of keeping the Union bound tightly together through any storm that might threaten it.

In 1847 he sided with President James K. Polk in favor of a piece of legislation that sought to make a territory of an enormous expanse of wilderness called the Oregon Country that had long been a source of contention between the United States and the United Kingdom, jointly occupied since a treaty signed in 1818 and finally sliced in half along the 49th parallel in a subsequent treaty in 1846. A year later the bill to create the Oregon Territory—the lower half of the area that had ended up in the possession of the United States—included a provision that slavery would be prohibited in the region and in any subsequent states into which it would be divided. Houston, by voting for the bill along with Thomas Hart Benton of Missouri, incurred the wrath of the rest of the southern senators, especially John C. Calhoun of South Carolina, their undisputed leader and a personal nemesis of Houston's for decades.

Their troubled relationship went back to 1818, when Houston, serving as a subordinate military Indian agent, had led a delegation of Cherokees to Washington to meet with President James Monroe regarding their traditional tribal lands in what is now the state of Arkansas. Houston, of course, was decked out in full Indian garb—including deer or buffalo skin leather leggings, feathers, and a brightly colored blanket worn as a cape.[2] When the Indians went in to see the president, Calhoun, then Monroe's secretary of war, told Houston to stay behind. When they were alone, he proceeded to castigate the twenty-five-year-old first lieutenant severely, leaving no doubt about his opinion of a soldier presenting himself to his commander in chief in such ridiculous primitive attire.[3] Even though Houston had recently submitted his resignation from his commission, he kept his temper during the tirade. But he never forgot it. Now, thirty years later, the two were squaring off again, but this time as equals.

Calhoun, an old veteran of decades of political wars, had served as a congressman, as vice president in the John Quincy Adams and Andrew Jackson administrations, and as secretary of both state and war before coming, in 1845, to the Senate to rule, with roaring oratory and an ominous, threatening scowl lodged beneath a wild shock of white hair, over what was by then called the "Southern Cause." Throughout the debate over Oregon, he made the issue of slavery his preeminent concern, leaving westward expansion for others to quibble with. If those future states out there in the wilds of the west all prohibited slavery, any representatives they sent to Congress would march in with a mandate detrimental to southern tradition and the bedrock of the southern economy. And this Calhoun and his brethren could not abide.

In his most stirring speech on the matter Senator Calhoun maintained that the author of the Declaration of Independence had erred when he proclaimed that all men are created equal. Jefferson, he professed, had taken "an utterly false view of the subordinate relation of the black to the white race in the South" when holding that the one, "though utterly unqualified to possess liberty, were as fully entitled to both liberty and equality" as the other and that to "deprive them of it was unjust and immoral." Calhoun surmised that this misguided belief, already set in stone as a tenet of the national consciousness, had surely led to "the deep and dangerous agitation which now threatens to engulf, and will certainly engulf, if not speedily settled, our political institutions, and involve the country in countless woes."[4]

Calhoun's take on the inequality of the races was well known even before he eloquently—and lengthily—espoused it, and Houston saw it as a moot point in regard to the bill in question. So he waved off the commotion over slavery that had been stirred up as pure foolishness. "I have no idea that slavery will ever be extended to that part of the United States," Houston said, having risen from his Senate desk, paying no attention to the tradition that first-term senators should not make speeches. "Nor do I have any idea that any person from the South . . . would desire to immigrate with his slaves to a region as inclement as that is, and incompatible as it is to [slave] labor."[5]

Throughout the debates Calhoun, who couldn't have cared less that cotton could not be grown in Oregon but cared a great deal that the eventual addition of several free states would tilt precariously the balance of power in Congress, regularly drew out a pair of his most useful weapons: the threatening, inflammatory phrases "nullification" and "secession," to which Houston once expressed his regret that the senator from South Carolina had used "menacing language" against the Union. Seemingly taken aback, Calhoun responded by saying he hadn't intended to be menacing, but he did see the need for a convention in which the South could chart its course. Houston replied, in a bit of waggishness that would be widely quoted, that he had personally experienced a few southern conventions, and on balance he had seen "a much more respectable convention of buffaloes."[6]

The Oregon Bill passed, bringing a huge new parcel of land (encompassing modern-day Oregon, Idaho, and Washington and portions of Montana and Wyoming) under the widening umbrella of the United States. It also moved Sam Houston further along on an independent, lonely path that he would follow for the rest of his life, usually at cross-purposes with his southern colleagues in the Senate, with the state legislature back home that had sent him there, and, ultimately, with a vast majority of the citizens of Texas.

• • •

By early 1850, just before Margaret Houston summoned her husband home, the tensions between the two political parties, Whigs and Democrats—fragmented even within themselves along sectional lines—had escalated to such an extent that it was beginning to look like nothing short of a miracle would prevent a complete parting of the ways between North and South.

The closest thing to a miracle available came in the person of Henry Clay of Kentucky, a longtime sage of the Whig Party and a persuasive orator, who had recently come out of retirement at the age of seventy-three for a last hurrah in Congress. It would prove to be a fortuitous decision for the nation and the brilliant culmination of a long, distinguished career.

Clay served in the House of Representatives several times (elected Speaker three times), served three previous terms in the Senate, was secretary of state in John Quincy Adams's second term, and waged unsuccessful presidential bids in 1824, 1832, and 1844. He returned to a Congress consumed by the raging debate between abolitionists and pro-slavery advocates, leaving those legislators hoping to find a path between them that might prevent a national calamity in a quickly narrowing middle ground.

What was needed, of course, was considerable give and take, and Clay was an old hand at such business. Thirty years previously, he had orchestrated the Missouri Compromise, which had settled the debate over slavery in the lands obtained in the Louisiana Purchase.[7] The deadlock had finally been broken by prohibiting slavery in the Great Plains region that is now the lion's share of the northern midsection of the continental United States, while permitting it in what would become the state of Missouri and in the Arkansas Territory.

Then, in 1848, the Treaty of Guadalupe Hidalgo between the United States and Mexico established the Rio Grande as the southern border of Texas and ceded all of California and an enormous parcel of land that would eventually become parts of Arizona, Colorado, Nevada, New Mexico, Utah, and Wyoming to the United States. Mexico, having suffered defeat in the Mexican-American War, had little choice but to grab the fifteen-million-dollar payment and call it a day. But with all that newly acquired land the Union bought further problems regarding just how the states that would fill it would regard slavery.

Now back home in the chamber he knew well, Clay started working through the points of contention as he saw them, primarily California's request to enter the Union as a free state and Texas already having been admitted as a slave state. Compounding the issue was a dispute over what Texas claimed were the boundaries of the old republic and that they expected to be the boundaries of the new state. The problem was these boundaries included a good bit of land already claimed by the United States: the eastern half of what is now the state of New Mexico, the panhandle of Oklahoma, a wide swath up through the midsection of what is now Colorado, and even bits of Kansas and southern Wyoming, all of which, if given to Texas, would allow slavery.

And there was an ongoing demand from the South to create a fugitive slave law to protect what southerners saw as personal property and demands from the North to bring an end to the buying and selling of slaves altogether, especially, as a matter of principle, in the nation's capital.

Senator Houston, ever insistent on holding the Union together, was as disgusted with one extreme viewpoint as the other and saw the need for cooler heads to enter the deliberation than those blowing all the current steam. In his 1849 reply to a letter from a former friend who had chastised him for opposing Calhoun during the Oregon debates, Houston went straight to what he perceived to be the heart of the problem. "In my humble opinion," he wrote, "the course pursued by Mr. Calhoun, and the Abolitionists, tend to the same end. So far they are co-workers and confederates. Could their designs be accomplished, the end would be the destruction of the Union."[8]

As early as January 6, before he received Margaret's New Year's Day letter dealing with happy children and imminent family visits, he mentioned Henry Clay in a dispatch to her. "As I have the floor for a speech tomorrow, I have no time to loose [*sic*], but must employ every hour. Mr. Clay concluded a speech of five hours, in two days," he wrote, probably more impressed with the subject matter than the length, which wasn't unusually long in that era. "His opinions, on various subjects, will meet opposition, by the south. He is currying favor with the north, and would like to have it with the south." Then he added, with his usual sprinkling of superfluous commas like salt and pepper on a plate of food, what appears to be something of a pledge of allegiance to Clay's cause. "If I should be fortunate, my intention is to direct my course to reconciliation, of sectional difficulties, and promoting the general prosperity of the Union, as a Union. Sectional policy must destroy the country, if persisted in, by either Party."[9]

But then, at about the time that Margaret would have received the letter and during the height of the compromise debates, she summoned Houston home to deal with problems in Huntsville that had nothing to do with free states, slave states, or boundaries.

Four

It wasn't uncommon, in that era of westering, for entire extended families to pull up roots and venture forth together to follow every afternoon's setting sun until they arrived at a new place and a new life. Such was the case with Nancy Lea's brood. During her first visit to the new republic in the fall of 1839, when she informed Houston that Margaret would not be coming to him to be married but he must go to her in Alabama, she had leased a house in Galveston, intending to run whatever business ventures she undertook from there.[1]

But Antoinette and William Bledsoe's sugar plantation at Grand Cane, some twenty miles north of the town of Liberty on the Trinity River, became the favored meeting place for all the transplanted and often visiting Leas. It was there, in early 1843, where Houston, then in his second term as president of the republic, had shamefully presented himself to relate his drunken battle with the bedpost to Margaret, who was visiting there during her pregnancy.

The Bledsoe's log house at Grand Cane was full at the time of that visit, with Margaret and Nancy Lea in residence along with her son Vernal and his wife, Mary. So Houston made a quick trip of it, taking his leave after receiving absolution from his magnanimous wife and returning to his presidential duties at Washington-on-the-Brazos.

While at Grand Cane Vernal and Mary Lea, on an excursion down to Galveston, encountered a child of seven whose parents had died in an outbreak of yellow fever. Having recently suffered the loss of an infant child and a miscarriage, they made inquiries and learned that the court was looking for a guardian for the little girl, who had no other family. Feeling it their Christian duty, and perhaps as a means to somehow soothe their double loss, they signed the necessary documents and took the girl back with them to Grand Cane to meet the family.[2] Thus, Virginia Thorne had come quite indirectly into Margaret's life. And her last name would, in time, unfortunately prove to be darkly prophetic.

By 1850, when Senator Houston made his hasty trip from Washington, his little family had been living in a comfortable new house in Huntsville for two years, their favorite of all the places they had called home since Margaret's arrival in Texas as a young bride. But getting there had proven to be a circuitous journey.

After their wedding in 1840 they sailed to Galveston and, eventually, across its wide bay to Cedar Point, a farm and tract of timber Houston owned on which a rough-hewn log cabin stood in various stages of completion. Margaret, barely twenty-one, surveyed the bleak structure and immediately elevated it in her mind by naming it Ben Lomond, which she remembered from one of her Sir Walter Scott novels.[3] It was a pretty name, and certainly Romantic. But Ben Lomond, a mountain of some three thousand feet in the windswept Scottish Highlands on the eastern shore of Loch Lomond, hardly fit this perfectly flat, humid, mosquito-infested landscape situated at less than one foot above absolute sea level. Today the property is gone completely, part of Galveston Bay.[4]

With the help of Eliza, the slave of about her own age who had been her childhood playmate and whom she inherited in her father's will, Margaret set up housekeeping. A year and a half later Houston was elected to his second term as president of the republic, replacing Lamar and inheriting the ruined economy his overspending had created. He and Margaret moved first to Austin and then, when Santa Anna's army raided nearby San Antonio, to Washington-on-the-Brazos where, after returning from her stay at Grand Cane, Margaret gave birth to Sam Houston Jr. in May 1843. His father proudly proclaimed the new arrival "robust and hearty as a Berkshire pig."[5]

Before his term was completed Houston purchased a plot of unimproved land on a hilltop surrounded by dense woodland thirteen miles east of the town of Huntsville, in Walker County, and sent Joshua, another slave Margaret had inherited from her father, to build a house there from plans drawn by Houston himself.[6]

In 1845 Houston, Margaret, and Sam Jr. moved into the two-room cabin of ax-squared logs, with puncheon floors, narrow open windows covered with plank shutters, and a chimney of stacked flat rocks.[7] The kitchen stood apart from the house. Their hill offered a fine view of the expansive countryside, but the trail up to the house was a tad steep and was often a muddy affair that required some trudging of both animals and humans.[8] They named the place Raven Hill, and Houston planned to retire there to the life of a gentleman farmer, probably intending to leave any actual sowing and reaping to Joshua and others. Still, just having him home would be the culmination of Margaret's hopes, prayers, and dreams.

At some point while they awaited the completion of the house, she penned a ten-stanza poem and left it on Houston's desk. She titled it "To My Husband," and her joy at the prospect of his homecoming from public responsibilities was her theme.

Dearest, the cloud has left thy brow,
The shade of thoughtfulness, of care
And deep anxiety; and now
The sunshine of content is there.

Near the end was a stanza that celebrated his putting the world and its problems behind him:

Thy task is done! Another eye
Than thine must guard thy country's weal;
And oh, may wisdom from on high
To him the one true path reveal.[9]

He might have believed the lines as he read them, and she might even have believed them as she wrote them. But the next year, when Texas was admitted to the United States, its first legislature sent a note up their hill to inform Houston he had been elected to represent Texas, along with Thomas Rusk, in the US Senate. Seeing it as his duty to go, and undoubtedly excited by the chance to step back into the limelight and the grandest political arena of them all, he accepted.

The life the Houstons had envisioned—the gentleman farmer tableau—quickly lost much of its appeal for Margaret when the farmer was over a thousand miles away most of the time. She soon concluded she needed closer access to medical care for the children—she had recently given birth to a daughter, Nancy Elizabeth (called Nannie by the family)—and for herself. Ashbel Smith, Houston's friend from the earliest days of the republic when he had appointed him surgeon general, had come up from Galveston to remove the tumor from her breast, with only a silver coin for her to bite down on to endure the pain since she refused to take even a drop of the whiskey he offered.[10]

She also needed a mercantile that did not require an overnight stay to trade with and, of course, a Baptist church in close proximity for comfort both spiritual and social. It must have been a lonely, sometimes frightening life for her, perched out in the middle of the wilderness with just her small children and a few slaves.

Having read this catalogue of misery more than once in her letters and fretting over it, Houston made something by way of a trade in 1847: a portion of Raven Hill for a small log cabin with a chimney made of mud and sticks on a piece of land considerably more attractive than its lone structure: two and a half acres on a hill gently sloping down to a pond, all of it a couple of miles south of the public square in Huntsville. A few months later he purchased an adjacent tract of 170 more acres, all forest and meadows. The first order of business had been to knock down the rough chimney and double the size of the cabin. Later, a second story was added.[11]

Perhaps wanting a structure that had his own unique stamp on it, as Washington, Jefferson, and Jackson had owned, Houston drew up the modifications and additions to the house himself. He had been a welcomed guest, practically a member of the family, several times at Jackson's Hermitage in Tennessee, and in 1823 as a young man just starting out in politics, he had presented a letter of introduction, written by Jackson, to eighty-year-old Thomas Jefferson at Monticello in Virginia.[12]

By 1847 Houston's name was already being tossed around as a possible presidential candidate in the next year's election, and adding his own homestead to those hallowed legacies would have been appealing to him, if not to Margaret, whose goal was still to bring him home for good to this little house rather than move with him into a much larger one on Pennsylvania Avenue in Washington.

His letters to her when the house was being constructed often contained instructions for the carpenters. In one he wrote that "if Mr. Royal should come to work on the chimneys, you can tell him to wall the foundations well. Make the hearths large, and the fire places to suit you. About five feet wide, and by all means well floored." He went on to send his regards to "mother"; Nancy Lea had by then entered into an amicable relationship with her son-in-law, though still maintaining what she considered to be her place in the chain of command. "You may have conquered Santa Anna," she is reported to have once told him only partly in jest, "but you shall never conquer me."[13] He ended the letter with "hugs and kisses" for the children and signed it "Thy Devoted, Houston." In the margin he scrawled an afterthought: "If necessary send for Mr. King to cut out the places for the chimneys."[14]

When it was finally completed, it was a practical, yet charming, white-washed house of two stories facing due north toward the courthouse and the town that was growing around it. Constructed of square-notched heart-pine logs covered with plank siding, it was at once pleasing to see from the road and still worthy of being technically called a log cabin when Houston needed to remind common folk that he was one of them. It had redbrick chimneys at each end, cedar shingles, and windows with real glass panes.

There was a wide, open area through the exact center on both levels, called a dogtrot on the ground floor and a breezeway on the second. The master bedroom and a parlor were on the first floor and two rooms where the children slept—Sam Jr. on one side, the girls on the other—directly above them. The breezeway where they played and, on stifling summer nights when mosquitoes weren't in residence, slept on pallets was enclosed by slender wooden balusters from the floor to the roof's overhang to keep the rambunctious Houston youngsters from tumbling out into the yard.

The parlor contained a round marble-top table and Margaret's piano—a gifted musician, she also played the harp and guitar—a red settee, and bookshelves filled with handsome bound volumes. The furniture in the master bedroom was more elegant than that in the children's rooms, where the growing horde required practical, sturdy pieces. There was even a quilting frame in the corner of Sam Jr.'s room because his mother had no other place to keep it. Hand-sewn mattresses made of blue-striped cotton ticking and stuffed with goose feathers were supported on all the bed-frames by ropes crisscrossed through holes in the sideboards. When the rope went slack and the mattress sagged, it had to be tightened with a bed key, a bulky wooden oblong device with a hole drilled through the bottom for the rope to be slipped through and a two-fisted auger-type handle at the top that, when turned, pulled the single length of rope taut so it could be tied off. Thus the origin of the wish that one might "sleep tight." The rest of the phrase—"and don't let the bedbugs bite"—alludes to the organic matter used to fill the mattresses, which often housed inhabitants other than feathers.[15]

All four rooms had fireplaces, none as large as the one in Eliza's free-standing kitchen, its deep firebox fixed with various iron hooks and swiveling brackets for hanging pots and kettles. A one-room log cabin housing Houston's law office sat in the northeastern corner of the yard; other out-buildings within the picket fence were a hen house, a smokehouse, and, in the outermost southwestern corner, the privy.

Outside the yard proper were a sprawling woodpile, small houses for the slaves and the overseer, the stable, a pen for the hogs, and a spring house close by a potato patch.[16] There were pecan and walnut trees, and Margaret planted fruit trees—apple, peach, fig, plum, and quince—in the front and filled four flower beds, two on either side of the walkway, with roses, lilacs, jonquils, narcissus, and lilies, stationing sixteen crepe myrtles as sentinels, one at the corner of each bed.[17] The myrtles' profusion of colorful blooms amid the backdrop of lush greenery made for a beautiful sight in spring and summer, their bare skeletal frames of smooth, glossy wood that appeared to have been polished just as alluring in fall and winter.

A white picket fence enclosed the entire yard with a gate at the front, another leading to a nearby spring from which slaves ferried containers of water, sometimes on their heads, for cooking and bathing, and one that opened into the vegetable garden that stretched the entire width of the yard out back.[18] There were bois d'arc trees and pomegranates and a couple of catalpas that Houston supposedly planted himself, perhaps his first use of a farming implement since tossing one down before running away to live with the Indians as a boy.

The property had been called Bermuda Farm when they bought it, which rang more agrarian than appealing. So they renamed it Woodland, which was a fitting name for what Margaret perhaps considered her first true home since leaving Alabama and the realization of her long-held hope of having a pleasant domicile in which to raise her children and share with her husband, who would soon be finally home from the looming tumult and winds of war outside her picket fence.

A decade before, in her first letter to him, she had described her brother's library in Marion as a sanctuary "untarnished by the wiles and cold deception of the world."[19] That assessment could as easily have defined Woodland, a place of happiness and peace, which it was, except for the fact that Virginia Thorne lived there.

Five

When Vernal and Mary Lea brought Virginia from Galveston to William and Antoinette's home at Grand Cane in 1843, she was seven, with brown eyes and chestnut hair.[1] No mention was ever made by those who remembered her about her being pretty, but even if she had been a raving beauty, it became clearly evident early on that her attitude and behavior could turn sour as quickly as a summer thunderstorm might billow up out of nowhere.

In no time at all she had locked horns with Nancy Lea, visiting there during Margaret's pregnancy. The sixty-two-year-old, always adept at controlling people—especially children—and events, apparently met her match in Virginia, who obstinately refused to be either threatened or governed. Nancy Lea attempted to take a switch to her at least once, but Vernal and Mary stopped her.[2]

Margaret had returned to Washington-on-the-Brazos shortly before the birth of Sam Jr., and her decision to go might have been hastened by the constant upheaval caused by the new addition to the household at Grand Cane. Mary Lea died not long after that. Then her husband, Vernal, asked his mother to take over the raising of Virginia, an unenviable task that for some reason fell to Margaret.

The ongoing problems between Margaret and Virginia over the next few years can be viewed in two lights. While the Houstons provided her a roof to sleep under, food to eat, and clothes to wear, it seems she was never seen as anything more than a servant, in essence just one more slave to be constantly ordered around by Eliza, who kept the slaves doing her bidding and attempted, with little or no success, to do the same with the belligerent girl. Virginia's moods turned even darker as time passed, and by 1850, she resented having to, in addition to her household and kitchen chores, tend to the needs of the three children and of Margaret, who was pregnant again.

The only person the angry child seemed able to confide in—more likely the only one who would pay her much attention—was the Houston's overseer, Thomas Gott. She complained, he listened, and their visits became a regular ritual. Huntsville being a small town, the time spent between a twenty-six-year-old man and a fourteen-year-old girl didn't go unnoticed for long. The gossip surely reached Margaret, but her difficulty with her fourth pregnancy and the subsequent melancholia she fell into had all but left her bedridden, depending on Eliza and her mother, in residence in her small bedroom off the back porch, for everything. So if Margaret heard complaints about Virginia and paid any attention to them, the matter would just have had to wait until the child arrived.

In Washington, Senator Houston might or might not have been aware of Virginia's new friendship. Margaret sometimes complained about the girl's bad attitude in her letters, and he, as early as 1845 in a couple of letters, warned Margaret to "watch with double vigilance. . . . Virginia is a fearful child . . . [and] there is no telling what the little monster will do."[3] Nevertheless, he had usually added greetings to Virginia in his litany of best wishes at the end of his own missives but exhibited no more interest in their unhappy charge than anyone else in the family had.

He was, however, concerned about Margaret's allusions to her current depression over her pregnancy. In a letter headed "Senate Chamber, 24th Jany, 1850," he told her, amid his usual parade of unnecessary commas, "So far as I can with delicacy, I have inquired, and I find, that Ladies are more distressed with the fourth child, than at any previous birth, and that the longer they have children, or the more they have, the more they are distressed in spirits."[4] The letter doesn't make clear whether this was intended to point out that nothing unusual was occurring, to cheer her up, or to imply that she wouldn't have to go through it again; however, they would have four more children after this one.

He ended the letter with some instructions about getting some exercise but to avoid going up and down the stairs. "If the weather is fine, you may exercise out of doors, but don't stoop any more than you can help. You may direct setting out flowers, but do not do it yourself."[5] Four days after he set down his orders, long before Margaret could have received them, she took pen in hand and warned Houston, in the middle of a lengthy letter, "You may prepare yourself for an astounding piece of news. On last night Virginia eloped with Gott, as I supposed to marry him, but today I learn he has taken her to Cincinnati [a town close to Huntsville] to go to school to Miss Rankin one session and then they are to marry."[6] Melinda Rankin, originally from New Hampshire, had come to Texas three years before with the intention of being a missionary to the Mexicans but ended up opening a school.

"You may form some idea of my astonishment by your own," Margaret continued, "for I was totally unprepared for it." She went on to say that Virginia had seemed more pleasant and happier of late and that she and the girl were "getting along finely," but, looking back on Virginia's devious behavior over the years, she concluded that it had all been a ruse leading up to this and that she had been "nursing a viper."[7]

All in all, she was ready to put the girl, the overseer, and the whole troubling business behind her. And good riddance. But she would find, in time, that fate doesn't always tie up its packages in such neat, convenient bundles.

Six

Huntsville was still in its infancy when the Houstons moved there. In the mid-1830s two brothers named Pleasant and Ephraim Gray petitioned the Mexican government to establish a settlement in northeastern Coahuila y Tejas to open a trading post with the peaceful Indians living in the vicinity and any white settlers who might wander in from the United States. When the application was approved, they set up shop on a relatively flat piece of land among the hills and glens that rose and fell through the area.[1]

Woodlands rich in game and an abundance of open prairie and rich river-bottom soil perfect for farming impressed pioneer families on their westward trek. And though there were few roads, more like trails, that offered easy navigation, there was the reliable Trinity River nearby accommodating vessels with shallow drafts headed down to Houston City and Galveston or north to new trading posts and settlements upriver.

When enough people, determining they had reached the end of their journey, built cabins and cleared and plowed fields, the Gray brothers decided the place needed a name. They chose Huntsville, after the town in Alabama where they had been raised.[2] One of the earliest descriptions of the new village was in the journal of William Bollaert, an Englishman who arrived in Galveston in February 1842 and traveled over the next two years, with notebook close at hand, through some of the wilderness and settlements within roughly a hundred miles of the coast of the Gulf of Mexico.

In what was perhaps the first visual depiction of Huntsville, Bollaert made a sketch on December 16, 1843, of a dozen or so small one-story and likely one-room cabins, some with chimneys and some without, on a flat landscape. In the foreground he delicately drew a few tall, sparse trees, so pale that the tip of his pencil must have barely touched the paper. To complete the scene, he added a couple of narrow structures that could only have been outhouses. Beneath his drawing he wrote, "Three miles brought us to Huntsville, situated on a pine height."[3]

A bit further on he recorded some of the businesses he passed: "Planter's Exchange, Gibbs Grocery, Huntsville Hotel, etc., etc.," and mentioned a brick store built by a Mr. McDonald with a Masonic Lodge on its upper floor and a "large brick building" for a boys and girls school that was under construction. In his own footnote, apparently inserted when his journal was later published in book form, he added, in contrast to his drawing of the little cluster of tiny cabins, that "the town consists of more than two hundred homes, a portion of which are built of brick" and that "building is going on and sound of the anvil and hammer heard continually."[4]

Huntsville stood as a fine example of new towns that cropped up on the expanding frontier of a nation that was marching westward. Most settlers fell into a spirit of camaraderie and civility, part of which they brought with them and part they honed once they arrived, born of the knowledge that they must depend on each other to survive.

"The houses in early Texas were small," Noah Smithwick, a blacksmith who came from North Carolina recalled, "but their hearts were large enough to cover all deficiencies. No candidate for hospitality was ever turned away. If there was a wedding everybody was invited and a long table set out in the yard, around which the guests stood while partaking of the cheer with which it was loaded. If the bridegroom had relatives they gave an 'infair' on the day following the wedding, at which the outdoor dinner was repeated."[5]

Another early transplant, John Salmon "Rip" Ford, who arrived in 1836 and eventually served his adopted home as a frontier doctor, Texas Ranger, and state senator, painted a fine portrait of the people who settled in towns like Huntsville. "A more candid, friendly and hospitable population never occupied any country," he wrote many years later. "A stranger was not allowed to pass a house without being invited to stop. No difference how long a guest remained, provided he minded his own business, he was entertained free of cost. If he asked for his bill, he was told a repetition of the inquiry would be taken as an insult. The coffee pot was on the fire at nearly every house in the country from daylight till bedtime. A visitor was invited to take a cup—a refusal was not taken in good part."[6]

By 1848, when Sam and Margaret hauled their three children and a dozen or so slaves—and Virginia Thorne, who seems to have fallen somewhere between the two groups—down from Raven Hill into town, Huntsville had grown into a lively community. Designated as the county seat of Walker County, it had a traditional public square on which a courthouse was being built. Houses, barns, blacksmith shops, stables, stores, and saloons began going up beside earthen streets laid out on a precise north-south grid and perpetually dusty or muddy, dependent on the weather, with enough exposed tree roots and stumps to shatter many a wagon wheel.[7]

Of the three inns in town that offered overnight accommodations to any travelers—if they were white, of course—but especially to a couple of stage lines that made regular stops, the largest was Pleasant Gray's Globe Hotel, which had a convenient artesian well out back that provided cool, clear drinking water. Two other, smaller, options were run by men named Keenan and Eutaw.[8]

Gibbs Mercantile, one of Huntsville's busiest centers of trade, would become a major fixture in the Houstons' lives. In fact, Margaret had already been a regular customer during her frequent trips into town from Raven Hill. Back in the early 1840s the founders of the business had purchased a lot at the intersection of Cedar and Jackson Streets—now Eleventh Street and Sam Houston Avenue—from Pleasant Gray, on the northwestern corner of the then-vacant public square awaiting its tardy courthouse. Thomas Gibbs, a native of South Carolina, and his partner, New Yorker Gardner Coffin, had arrived in Huntsville with the items that made up their initial inventory, confident that Gibbs and Coffin Mercantile would eventually open somewhere.[9]

Later, when Gardner Coffin died, Thomas Gibbs paid Coffin's father for the half interest in the outfit that had been left to him.[10] Then he persuaded his brother Sandford to come in with him, and the name was changed to Gibbs Brothers, which is today the oldest company in Texas operating in the same location under the same ownership, according to the descendants of several generations of Gibbses. Though it hasn't sold a bag of flour or a tin of tobacco in many a year, the company now oversees a massive portfolio of landholdings and investments that started growing even before Gardner Coffin died, when Texas had been a republic.

By 1850 the store was a hub of enterprise and a beehive of activity, its various wares spilling out onto the plank walkway through the front door that faced the finally finished courthouse. However, after such a long wait, the courthouse was completely razed just three years later and replaced, its foundation proving too weak to support it.

Gibbs Brothers was a "general store" of the sort that most of America depended on in the mid-nineteenth century, offering cooking utensils, farming implements, wide bolts of fabric sold by the yard, a limited selection of shoes and clothing (mostly thick, sturdy wear for farm work), various medicines like castor oil and sundry tonics and elixirs, and a line of glass jars full of hard candies that youngsters lusted after on trips into town. There were some fruits and vegetables in season, but most folks depended on their own trees and gardens for those. Always in supply were heavy cloth bags of flour, sugar, coffee, salt, corn meal, and a huge cracker barrel that did double duty as something to lean on while getting the latest gossip.[11]

The Gibbs Brothers eventually operated a small bank in the rear of the store and in 1890, with several Huntsville business leaders, opened Gibbs National Bank. But in Sam Houston's time the mercantile itself served as a ready source of cash loaned at a fair interest rate, with transactions entered into a huge, cloth-covered ledger the size of the top of a small side table. It wasn't uncommon for Sam or Margaret to withdraw funds in gold, silver, or notes.

The Houstons did most, if not all, of their trading with the Gibbses. In the ledger for 1852, under the heading "Genl. Sam Houston," the following entries appear with many, many more written out in sweeping, ornate calligraphy flowing across tall lined pages, now brown and brittle after more than 160 years.

1 silver thimble—50 cents
6½ #s crushed sugar—$1.00
3 sps. thread—10 cents
Cash to Houston—$100.00
1 saddlebag—$5.00
1 pr. Lady's shoes—$1.25
Gloves (2)—80 cents
5 balls cord—15 cents
Cash to Houston—$135.00[12]

Over the years that the family lived in Huntsville the pages in Gibbs's ledgers titled either "Genl. Sam Houston" or "Honl. Sam Houston" recorded numerous withdrawals designated for specific people whose names precede the amount. Apparently those funds were given over in cash to be taken to whomever needed to be paid for services rendered.

The Gibbs Brothers, who provided practically everything else, didn't offer personal checking.

There are also some entries that were obviously payouts *to* the Houstons. In 1856 these appear: "Feb. 21, Cash pd. for potatoes—$1.50" and "Feb. 28, Cash pd. for onions—50 cents." So Eliza's garden must have been one of several in town that provided fresh produce for the store's green grocery bins. On the first day of July of that year a ball of cord set the household back a nickel. The price of cord had gone up since 1852, when five balls went for fifteen cents.

The Gibbs Brothers' ledgers provide a unique window into the daily lives and needs of a growing family in an antebellum small town in what was still basically a wilderness. There is page after page of purchases of shoes, nails, lengths of fabric, basic foodstuffs—including an abundance of sugar; the Houstons were especially fond of the cakes, pies, and sweet cakes that were consistently brought in from Eliza's outside kitchen—and more than a few items that defy modern recognition. The old, heavy books relate a fascinating story, all penned in forward-leaning, sharp-pointed letters and numerals undulating like a lake's waves on a blustery day.

The relationship between Sam Houston and Thomas Gibbs grew into a close personal friendship, so close that Houston named him an executor of his will and even presumed to ask him to see to the welfare of his children should Margaret die before they all reached adulthood.[13]

More and more stores and businesses opened along the crisscrossing streets of the growing town, and diarist William Bollaert's "sound of the anvil and hammer" was still evident as new houses and barns emerged. Some mighty impressive buildings were going up, several adorned with the ornate embellishments consistent with the architectural style becoming known as Victorian.

One new structure, more classical than Victorian, had yet to be completed. Austin College would be a stately two-story redbrick edifice housing a Presbyterian school for young men, most of whom intended to become ministers. It eventually had four imposing white Tuscan-style columns on the north side and four more on the south. Crowned with an imposing cupola, the tip of which reached seventy feet, it sat atop Capitol Hill, so called because Huntsville had recently hoped to be chosen as the site of the state legislature and townsfolk had envisioned the capitol building sitting there.[14]

The Houston's home was just down the hill and across the road, which was convenient for the senator when he was in town; it was a short walk up the hill to attend meetings as a member of the school's first administrative board. The front of the college looked north, down its hill to the back of the state penitentiary in town.

The Walls had been there for two years in 1850, so large a prison that it had to be built across a long section of the street later named for Sam Houston. This seems somehow appropriate since he figures into one of the many tales that have drifted down the years about the place. In 1848, according to the story, when the precise perimeters of the future prison's walls were being marked off by surveyors, a sizable group of Huntsville's citizens, including men, women, and children, congregated to watch the men at their task one early morning. A few of the men had fought at San Jacinto just a dozen years before. Some had lost friends or relatives at the Alamo. Those who hadn't recently drifted in from the east had been citizens of the United States, then Mexico, then the Republic of Texas, and now the United States again. But all of that meant little, when weighed against getting in a crop, or cutting timber, or selling enough goods in their stores to provide for their families.

The story goes that Sam Houston was there too, having just moved to town himself and home from the Senate during a recess, leaning on the walking stick that he always carried. Supposedly somebody wandered over to him wanting to know if the rumor going around was true, about how Huntsville getting the prison—which was indeed a plum, no argument there—had taken them out of the running for being picked as the permanent site of the state capital and the legislature.

Houston is supposed to have leaned on his stick and probed at some pine straw and twigs with the toe of one boot. He usually took longer to give a reply or actually do a thing than most people were happy with; letting Santa Anna chase his army across the state to San Jacinto before finally turning and fighting had cost him a deluge of criticism, most of it from his own men—until they won the battle, of course.

Finally, Houston is supposed to have said that he had at various times in his life been associated with several legislatures. And that, on balance, the town would likely be getting a better grade of people in a prison. Maybe he was there; maybe he wasn't. Maybe he said it, and maybe not. The old story—like the one from the next century that is told by many who lived in Huntsville during the era when condemned convicts were executed in the Walls' electric chair about every light in town going dim when the switch was thrown—are part of the rich fabric of the place.

The electric chair used during the middle decades of the twentieth century was, in fact, powered by its own generator, and no lights would have dimmed even in the room where it sat.[15] And there is no record of Sam Houston having been in attendance when the surveyors did their work. But the stories became legends, and the legends eventually became facts. In Texas, legends and facts often weave their way amicably beside each other through the state's history.

Huntsville, in 1850, was growing into itself, becoming the town that it would, in many respects, remain for the next century and a half. For the most part, people liked what they saw when they visited. They still do. But at least one traveler that year determined that an essential element necessary for the town's success was not yet fully in place. Melinda Rankin, the schoolteacher in nearby Cincinnati to whom Thomas Gott had taken his fourteen-year-old fiancée Virginia Thorne for a short stab at formal education, was putting the finishing touches on a book.[16]

Her original intention to become a missionary to the Mexicans had to be rerouted upon her arrival three years earlier. The Mexicans—Roman Catholic to a man, woman, and child—were not about to be proselytized or preached to by a no-nonsense Scottish Presbyterian New England woman. So she had become a schoolmarm.

After taking up her new profession she fell ill, not dangerously so, and during her convalescence she wrote most of a manuscript to which she gave the bland yet succinct title *Texas in 1850*. Published in that year, when Virginia was one of her students, it related a brief history of the recent revolution and her observations on several towns that she had visited. It was less almanac or tour guide than a blatant appeal to religious workers back east to flock to the new state that she felt was greatly in need of spiritual revival.[17]

As a tour guide it would have been a disappointment anyway since she found, more often than not, little that sufficiently impressed her to recommend anyone go touring. She did say, early on, that Texas possessed "a climate as mild as far-flung Italy"[18]—she had obviously never been to Italy—but she offered not very much about local customs or interesting facts and an abundance of condemnation regarding too few churches and, in regard to moral standards, too great a distance from what she perceived as the only true path for civilized people to march along. "The worth of the Puritan system," she wrote in the first chapter, "is already recorded on the page of history, and may, with propriety, be referred to as a controlling element of power in the development and progress of society."[19]

She must have located at least a smattering of that moral righteousness in Huntsville (the current construction of Austin College, a Presbyterian preacher mill, surely would have been gratifying). In the six pages she devoted to the fledgling town she found at least some faint hope that it might eventually make something of itself: "A concentration of talent, enterprise and morality is proven by the history of Huntsville," she said, "and the rapid improvement under the circumstances speaks much in favor of its future prosperity."[20]

But Melinda Rankin believed all that talent and energy had not yet found its proper direction. "In the eagerness of the citizens of Huntsville to ornament the town with public buildings, churches have been, evidently, overlooked." She went on to state that the Baptists are the "most numerous" of what believers were there and that "the Cumberland and Old School Presbyterians have each organized churches within the last two years,"[21] which must have pleased the Presbyterian teacher who was still very much a missionary at heart.

But she was far from won over. "The demands for Huntsville," she believed, "are for an enlightened, earnest and consistent Christianity. The refinement and intelligence of the people demand it, the intense aspirations for worldly distinction demand it, else the voice of God will be drowned 'in the tumult of the sea of life.'"[22]

One voice probably not being drowned out in Rankin's school was that of young Virginia Thorne. Anyone who had stood down the formidable Nancy Lea and helped put her daughter Margaret in bed, exhausted and depressed, was not likely to have been intimidated by a mere Yankee schoolteacher.

Seven

In the first months of 1850 the broadsheets from Washington, New York, Boston, and Philadelphia that Senator Sam Houston would have perused in his rented room in the nation's capital would, in addition to providing blow-by-blow accounts of the impassioned Senate debate over Clay's compromise bill, have been full of all manner of other goings-on in the world.

In London a parliamentary duel pitting foreign intervention against isolationism, an argument the United States would take up in earnest toward the end of the century, was as volatile as the current compromise harangue in Washington. The English clamor was over the much-discussed Don Pacifico affair, a three-year-old web of political intrigue, injustice, and religious persecution—a heady mixture fetching worldwide interest—involving a gentleman of Portuguese Jewish descent who, as a resident of Gibraltar, was technically a British subject.

In 1847, while serving in Athens as a consul representing Portugal, David Pacifico had been attacked and robbed by a pack of anti-Semitic ruffians, at least one of whom was the son of a high-ranking Greek statesman. Pacifico's demand that Greek authorities hunt down the thieves and recover his possessions, some of which were official Portuguese documents, or at least compensate him in some way for his loss, went continuously unheeded. Finally, he appealed to England, whose foreign secretary, Lord Palmerston, figuring the bright sun of the British Empire should shine on its distant subjects in any land, imposed an embargo on the Greek port of Piraeus, igniting a standoff between those in the government who viewed gunboat diplomacy as the most noble option and those who saw staying out of the whole mess as the most prudent. It continued for some months, until Greece finally offered some little recompense, apparently enough to soothe everyone's feathers.

Houston would likely have read the Pacifico dispatches closely. Given England's inclination to expand its vast empire to widespread corners of the globe, he had, when president of the Republic of Texas, apparently courted the prime minister and parliament when negotiating annexation as a state, probably teasing the president and Congress with the possibility of ending up with a British colony at their back door.

Every edition of every paper offered a veritable smorgasbord of interesting tidbits. The University of Utah opened its doors in Salt Lake City, and in California, the wellspring of much of the turmoil in the compromise debate, gold was still being taken from streams, rivers, mines, and—according to some reports—from the surface of the ground itself in staggering quantities. Future stagecoach impresarios Henry Wells and William Fargo launched a freight-hauling enterprise called, patriotically enough, "American Express." A patent was granted for an "adding machine" that had keys corresponding to numerals that could be pressed down to somehow magically reckon sums. There was growing interest in a new process called dry cleaning that had recently been discovered when one M. Jolly-Bellin accidentally tipped over a lamp, spilling a mixture of oil and turpentine on a pile of soiled clothing, instantly removing stains without soap or water. And an original handwritten copy of George Washington's 1796 farewell address sold at auction for twenty-three hundred dollars, roughly equivalent to seventy thousand in today's economy.[1]

A posed daguerreotype of showman Phineas Taylor Barnum and his most famous attraction, Charles Sherwood Stratton, known to the world as General Tom Thumb, was printed regularly in papers. The little general, twelve years old and less than three feet tall, outfitted in starched white trousers, a tight vest under a short military cutaway jacket, and a visored cap tilted cockily on his tiny head, stood ramrod straight, one spit-shined shoe crossed nonchalantly over the other, on a chair with one hand on Barnum's shoulder. Given Houston's appreciation of colorful attire, he might have enjoyed the photograph, and he would have seen it often (Barnum undoubtedly had an excellent press agent).

Houston would have probably passed over booksellers' advertisements for a new novel by Nathaniel Hawthorne called *The Scarlet Letter*. But he might have read of the departure from Plymouth, England, of a group of explorers off to the icy Artic in search of an earlier expedition missing there while attempting to locate what might or might not be the nearly mythical Northwest Passage. If that fabled conduit actually existed connecting the northern Atlantic and Pacific Oceans, it would provide an enormous boon to global navigation and trade. At fifty-seven, Houston still retained enough wanderlust and sense of adventure to feel the tug of a frontier as vast and daunting as that.

In Huntsville Margaret would have seen few if any of these things. Her reading was confined pretty much to the King James Bible, certain Baptist devotional tracts, and, in her weaker moments, to old friends from her youth like *Ivanhoe*, *The Bride of Lammermoor*, *Rob Roy*, and occasional verses by Poe, Longfellow, and Tennyson. Current events and politics held little interest for her; in fact, she considered the whole notion of vying for high office and climbing the ladder of political power and influence as dangerously flirting with pomposity.

In February 1848, Houston, having been in Washington for two years and a frequent guest in the whirlwind of social gatherings, attended a White House dinner in honor of eighty-year-old former first lady Dolly Madison. Late that night he wrote to Margaret about the evening. "I made some display by asking Mrs. President Polk to take my arm, and we walked around the 'East Room.' There [was] a vast crowd of people there, and they were gratified as it seemed, that I was so gallant a man!" Full of recent impressions, and not a little of himself, he went on. "I only regret, that you were not upon my arm. . . . I would infinitely prefer to have you, than any one on earth. I suppose that not less, than one hundred persons of both sexes, spoke to me on the subject of bringing you to the White House, & living there! It may be so!"[2]

Having navigated through that barrage of commas and pretention Margaret might have felt the need to fire off a response encapsulating her views on both strutting through the presidential mansion and the prospect of moving into it. But she didn't have to, since she'd covered the territory already; in a letter dated February 15, before Houston's note reached her she had left no doubt regarding her aversion to putting on airs. "I cannot enter into the schemes of worldly greatness," she wrote, "which your friends are planning for you. Should the Lord have work for you to do, I know he will direct you, but the praise of man is an empty thing, and one year of domestic quiet is worth all the laurels of earthy heroes' fame."[3] She was perfectly content to be inside her picket fence and out of the public eye. Little did she realize that very soon much of the news in Huntsville, falling far afield of the interest of the national and international press, would center around Virginia Thorne, Thomas Gott, and, most concerning of all, herself.

• • •

Houston had originally intended to stay in Washington until the summer recess, especially given the ongoing floor debates and constant backroom meetings over Senator Clay's compromise proposals. But Margaret, having a more difficult time with this pregnancy than the previous three, had suggested in her letters, in no uncertain terms, that she preferred that he make a visit, however brief, before then.

She was also worried about the management of the farm, that duty having fallen, since the abrupt departure of Thomas Gott with Virginia, to a cantankerous fellow named Anthony Hatch. "The old man," Margaret wrote to Houston in early February, "is naturally obscene and illnatured [*sic*] and must have an object on which to vent his spleen."[4] He particularly disliked her mother, who became the most constant recipient of his foul-mouthed ire. Nancy Lea surely prayed for him—her religion would have mandated that—but she likely also sent up requests that the family might soon be rid of him.

"I think you will find that Mr. Hatch does not know much about hogs," Margaret wrote in late January, a couple of paragraphs after informing Houston of Virginia's and Gott's elopement and not yet fully aware of the old man's acerbic nature or his ineptitude, "but never mind we shall have aplenty, and I merely mention this to prepare you for a dissappointment [*sic*], when you get home."[5]

More concerning to Houston than Margaret's worrisome pregnancy and the unpleasant farm manager was what was becoming more and more evident in her letters of a deepening depression. "It may be that I have done wrong to insist on your coming," she wrote in mid-February, "but I trust it will be for the best. When I did so, it was under the melancholy impression that I should not survive the spring, and even now I am not free from apprehensions, but my health is much improved, and my cough has almost left me altogether."[6]

Concluding that nothing short of delivering himself in person would boost Margaret's morale and quell her worries, Houston wrote that he would try to come home for a short visit in the spring. Margaret replied that she "would have no objection" to the ninth of May, which would be the tenth anniversary of their marriage. But she probably hoped that it would be sooner. It would be.

His need to see Margaret and to set things right in Huntsville, coupled with his absolute intention to be back at his desk to cast his vote in favor of the compromise bill late in the session, convinced him to make the trip as soon as possible. But first he had just one essential task to complete before he could leave Washington. He had to give the most important speech of his Senate career thus far.

• • •

On February 8, a Friday, the public galleries of the chamber were so packed that the rules were suspended and some of the overflow crowd was allowed to stand on the Senate floor. One account of the day recorded that ladies sat on stools between the senators' desks.[7] The narrow, steeply inclined upper galleries were stuffy and cramped, offering little in the way of comfort and leg room; it wasn't uncommon for senators and their aides to lift up refreshments on long sticks to family members and their guests wedged in up there.[8]

The debates over Senator Clay's compromise bill had drawn larger-than-average crowds, but the attendance was especially high today because the hero of San Jacinto was to take the floor. People turned out for a hero, especially one who cracked wise on occasion and often dressed in colorful get-ups. And for this speech, he had been not only the author but his own publicist. After working the text of his address through several drafts until he had the one he was most satisfied with, he had sent advance copies to several editors and reporters.

Of the papers that printed parts of the speech and their opinions of it the Boston *Post* offered one of the most concise, accurate previews of what the senator from Texas would say:

> General Sam Houston speaks tomorrow. He, too, will make a Union speech, calm, patriotic, and becoming the brave and heroic senator who represents the youngest child of the American Union. It is said that "Sam" means to attack Calhoun. He will not do so. He will merely defend himself from the aspersions thrown upon his views in regard to the slavery question. Sam is no fanatic either way; and seeks no remedy for the evils under which the South are now laboring in disunion and anarchy. He will insist on the constitutional rights of the South; and he will ask nothing more.[9]

So the stage was set for high drama in the ornate semicircular chamber beneath its half dome and single chandelier. The senator's desks—narrow, upright structures with steep-slanted tops not unlike students' stations in schools—formed a half circle facing a looming canopy, its heavy scarlet drapery gathered back by golden ropes and dropping down to the floor. A tall cushioned armchair sat beneath the impressive structure, occupied almost always by someone other than Millard Fillmore, who as vice president of the nation was the also president of the Senate. Neither lofty position would have required him to do much of anything; he could cast a vote in the Senate only if he was called on to break a tie, and as vice president he would have been given only a few ceremonial duties to carry out. He wouldn't have long to wait for a promotion, however; exactly five months and one day later Zachary Taylor would suddenly die of cholera—or a spoiled snack of cherries and milk; accounts vary[10]—and Fillmore would become the thirteenth president. The fierce golden eagle that thrust itself forward from the peak of the canopy stared threateningly out at the assembled crowd, its squinted beady eyes seeming to make sure that the business of democracy was being properly conducted.

When all was quiet in the room, the great gavel was pounded and "the junior senator from Texas" was recognized to speak. Since both senators from the new state had arrived together in 1846, they had drawn lots to see who whose term would be a full six years and who would have to face reelection by the state legislature in two.

Once on his feet Houston would have taken his time before beginning. He was a great taker of time, either to be sure of his course, as he had when running away from Santa Anna's army before facing it, or for dramatic effect when addressing a crowd. When he finally commenced, his voice low enough at first to make the cramped congregation in the gallery lean in closer to better hear him, he waded slowly through a bit of cordial pleasantry and a self-deprecation, devices often employed by speakers before stirring whatever pot they intend to stir. "However incompetent I may be," he said, feeling completely competent, "I feel that it is my duty to offer my views in a respectful, frank, and candid manner, as the representative of that state whose interests are involved in the resolutions offered for our consideration."[11]

Texas had much at stake. A crucial component of Senator Clay's bill would, if approved by the Texas legislature, in one fell swoop wipe clean the state's massive war debt from its revolution, at the cost of narrowing its borders significantly. But Houston saw the compromise package as much more important than its impact on one state or even one region. He believed, truly believed, it was the last viable chance of avoiding a civil war.

He dealt with the issue of slavery first, restating unequivocally his belief that Congress had no power to impose any restrictions regarding that institution on the states. "Nor do I believe that congress has, under the Constitution, any authority to impose upon states asking for admission into the Union any condition whatever, other than that of having a republican form of government." This wouldn't have come as a surprise to anyone. As an unwavering Jacksonian Democrat from the moment that Jackson himself had looked down at him from his horse during the War of 1812, he saw true power as emanating only from the people themselves, through the legislatures of their individual states.

"We do not ask the North to concede anything," he said, speaking for the moment for the whole South, though he was diametrically opposed to their threats to bolt from the Union. "We merely ask them to abstain from aggression. The South only asks that her rights be respected in relation to the Constitution of the United States, by which all states are bound."

While the full gallery paid rapt attention to his every word and his fellow senators sat stoically, knowing the words before he delivered them, Houston issued the plea that was the crux of his message: "I call upon the friends of the Union from every quarter to come forward like men, and to sacrifice their differences upon the common altar of their country's good, and to form a bulwark around the Constitution that cannot be shaken."

Then he took up a theme that he would often return to for the rest of his life: a warning of what a civil war would actually entail for common folk with little or no interest in politics. He asked the Senate to think of those people when "you carry it [war] to the hearths of the farmer, the mechanic, who has every comfort of life around him . . . and tell him 'you now have to encounter . . . the worst of all wars, not of race . . . or of religion, but a war of brothers.'" The reference to farmer and mechanic was no accident, of course. In one swift brushstroke he painted both regions—agrarian South and industrial North—in the image he wished to convey: everyday citizens caught in the lunacy of war.

After invoking blessings for the Union, asking that "he who buildeth up and pulleth down nations" to bring unity, he pilfered a line from the Gospel of Mark: "For a nation divided against itself," he said near the end, with sufficient emphasis to make it a very real threat, "cannot stand."

Out in Illinois a tall, lanky, former one-term congressman who had returned to his law practice might have underlined that snippet of scripture when he read the text of the speech in the newspaper. For eight years later Abraham Lincoln would have reason to trot it out again.

• • •

Over the next couple of days Houston informed his colleagues that he would have to be gone for a while, giving illness in the family as the only reason and promising to make his absence as brief as possible. Then he went home to Margaret.

Eight

Whether or not Houston's showing up in Huntsville came as a complete surprise is unknown. The surviving letters that he posted to Margaret from Washington prior to his departure made no mention of his decision to come so soon, and even if he had notified her, he might have actually arrived before his letter did. Mail delivery was an iffy enterprise at best; if it showed up at all, it was painfully slow.

Once at home he quickly took matters in hand. He hired a man named Daniel Johnson to manage the farm and oversee the slaves.[1] So the bellicose Anthony Hatch was either sent packing or demoted. Johnson had to be apprised of things that needed doing, some just once and others as regular maintenance. And he had to be told which hogs to fatten and sell and which ones would end up in the smokehouse as sausage in barrels and as hams and slabs of bacon over the slow-burning fire in the fall.

And there would have been the matter of how much corn to plant. There's no evidence that the farm yielded vast acres of cash crops, but corn was an absolute necessity, a completely consumable resource for every living creature on the place, human and animal. In addition to its being served as roasting ears at the humans' table and scattered out for chickens and in troughs for the livestock, it was the base ingredient in grits, chowders, pudding, succotash, popcorn, and, of course, cornbread, a constant staple at many meals that would be the primary source of nutrition for the Confederate army a decade later.[2] Corncobs were used for fertilizer, fuel, and smoking pipes and even the shucks for dolls, mattress filling, and toilet tissue.[3]

The big garden behind the yard was probably entirely Eliza's bailiwick, and she—not either of her masters or her overseer—would have determined which of its rows would be planted with various leafy and root vegetables and which slaves would keep them weeded, watered, and harvested. Houston would have made a thorough inspection of fences, pathways, and the house and outbuildings themselves to see if any repairs were in order or any loose cedar shingles needed replacing. In town, the account ledgers at Gibbs Mercantile and other establishments had to be checked over and a bevy of townsfolks' questions answered regarding the compromise bill and other congressional business.

There was likely a flurry of congratulations from his supporters on his recent speech, the text of which would have been published verbatim in Texas newspapers and posted in the windows of various businesses and at the courthouse. Conversely, a growing faction opposed what they saw as his willingness to give away too much of the state in the border compromise and of cozying up to northerners, Whigs, and abolitionists, each of which an average resident of Huntsville would have considered vile.

One of the strongest voices in the anti-Houston camp belonged to Louis Wigfall, a state representative from Marshall whom Houston believed was much influenced by his old adversary David Burnet, the interim president of Texas during the revolution, who saw any compromise between North and South as unlikely as it would have once been between Tejas and Mexico.[4]

Many of the same papers that printed the text of Houston's speech also offered considerably harsh editorial ranting, beneath broad headlines on their front pages, regarding his leaving his post in the midst of the compromise debates, especially since the California amendment was due to come up for a vote soon. Houston brushed it all aside, maintaining that nothing of importance could transpire in Washington before his return and that Senator Rusk was seeing to Texas' interests in his absence.[5]

He spent much of his time during his stay of several weeks in the one-room log cabin law office in the corner of the yard at Woodland seeing some of his clients and spending hours with his close friend Henderson Yoakum, a fellow lawyer who tended to Houston's practice in his absence. Yoakum, a West Point graduate, had served in the Tennessee Senate before moving to Texas in 1845 and, in addition to maintaining his law practice, was working on what became a two-volume history of Texas from its earliest settlements to its annexation as a state.

Men from town who just dropped by for a chat ended up not in the house's parlor but out in the law office. It was a comfortable room—a man's room—with walls of dark horizontal rough-cut logs separated by narrow lines of white pitch. There were bound law books in cases; a writing table covered with documents, candlesticks, a pewter inkwell, several quill and metal pens; and probably a small glass of orange peels muddled into bitters, the concoction Houston, a reformed drinker, swore kept him from falling off the precarious wagon he had stayed on for almost a decade. Slender ladder-back chairs with seats of crisscrossed rope were arranged in a circle in the middle of the room, a brass spittoon or two situated conveniently. It being late February, flames might have steadily licked away at a few logs in the fireplace.

Houston probably attended at least one meeting of the administrative board of the newly created Austin College, and he no doubt did considerable glad-handing around town. For, much as Margaret wanted him out of politics, he would have half an eye cast down the road; his name popped up in too many presidential calculations to be otherwise.

During his stay he would make sure that his slaves were provided for, that they had warm clothing and were well shod; "one pr. Shoes" for one slave or another appeared regularly in the Gibbs ledger pages for the Houston household. Though he was adamant that slavery was an essential component in the agrarian infrastructure of the South, he never defended it as a morally right practice. And there is no evidence that he was ever cruel to his slaves or that he allowed his overseers to be. He forbade whipping, and Margaret made sure the slave quarters were kept clean and plenty of blankets provided. Houston allowed Joshua to keep the wages he was paid for doing carpentry jobs for people in town, not a common practice, and he even taught him to read, which was at the time a violation of state law.[6]

This is all shallow support for his keeping human beings in bondage, to be sure. Nor is it intended to be any sort of defense for his actions. But in an era and a geographical location where slavery was a given, Houston was by all accounts one of the exceptions to the sometimes common stereotype of the cruel, whip-snapping taskmaster.

Of course, he would have spent an abundance of his time with Sam Jr., Nannie, and Maggie, telling the children stories and giving them whatever little gifts he had brought for them from Washington. He would have quizzed Sam Jr. on his lessons and told him to be good to his mother and his sisters, and to his grandmother, who was currently on especially good terms with her son-in-law, possibly because he had dispatched the foul Anthony Hatch.

Houston pinned high hopes on his firstborn and namesake, pushing him always to study hard and behave himself. Three weeks after his son's birth the proud, hopeful father had written to Charles Elliott, the British chargé d'affaires for the Republic of Texas, that he hoped his son would "be anything but a loafer, an agitator, or, in other words, a demagogue."[7] He would often urge Margaret to steer the boy clear of wasting time reading novels and, above all, from dallying in writing poetry, lest he become a dreamy versifier like Mirabeau Lamar. Early on Houston had expressed the hope that Sam Jr. would not grow up to be a poet or a "singer of songs."[8]

In 1845, when Sam Jr. was barely two years old, his father held him up to look at the corpse of Andrew Jackson and told him to try to remember him. The Houstons, on a trip to Tennessee, had hurried to the Hermitage to visit the ailing Jackson, but he died shortly before their arrival. In putting his young son in close proximity to such greatness, he must have figured, some of it might somehow instill itself in him.[9]

Houston had recently promised Sam Jr. a sword if he did well in his studies, not a common enticement in modern times for a seven-year-old but perhaps not unusual for that era or for the son of a general. He gave him a choice of a brand-new sword with his name inscribed on it or the one with which he had led the charge at San Jacinto.[10] In a letter from Margaret that was traveling toward Washington as Houston was making his way home, she passed on Sam Jr.'s request for "a box of magnetized fish" to be used with a metal hook on a fishing line.[11] But his son would have to make do with a real sword, possibly one of the most important ever wielded in American history.

All in all, Houston had plenty to do and many people to talk to during his sojourn from the Senate. But before he did any of those things, he would have made sure of Margaret. First and foremost, he would have had to convince himself that she was getting better and that her emotions were in check. Of course, the simple fact that he was home would have cheered her up considerably, but there was no assurance that she would not again sink into despair once he left again.

This pregnancy was, indeed, proving more difficult than the earlier ones. So there were none of the long walks together that she so enjoyed, but there were surely nights by the fire in the parlor or in their bedroom, her reading him something from the Bible or a bit of poetry. If she grew tired, perhaps he would have read something to her, maybe wondering to himself why the author—be it the Apostle Paul or Alfred, Lord Tennyson—was so miserly with his commas.

There might have been some late-winter gloamings: Margaret in the rocker in the breezeway or out on the lawn—a shawl over her shoulders, a light blanket over her legs—her husband close enough to touch in the chair beside her, Sam Jr. sprinting after the first fireflies as darkness swallowed up the day's last light, Nannie and Maggie chasing him across the yard, cackling like hens.

Margaret, as uncomfortable as she was, must have savored every moment of those days. For her contentment depended in large part on Houston being within her reach. As the date for his departure drew close, she had to face the realization that he would once again not be present for the birth of a new addition to the family. He was there for a time, and that would have to suffice. She had—like Abigail Adams, another good wife of another public figure who was absent for frequent long spells—learned to count other blessings.

In the last letter Margaret posted to Houston before his arrival, which he would not read until he was back in Washington, she expressed a sentiment that was a running motif in all of her missives: "I am living in great hopes of seeing you shortly."[12] Her greater hope, of course, was that he would soon leave the Senate and public life for good, trading the large world for her much smaller one.

She had started the letter on February 24, 1850, by mentioning that she was writing it late at night so she could deliver it to someone who was leaving for Washington early the next morning. At the end she wrote, "Good night dearest," as if he were actually there bedside her. Then she inscribed the same tiny, neatly penned gathering of three words above her signature that she used to close most of her notes to him: "Thy devoted wife." Never, it would seem, have truer words been written.

Nine

He left in mid-March, beginning the several-weeks' journey back to the nation's capital. He passed some of it, wherever his various conveyances stopped for the night, by writing several letters home and posting them with stages heading west. So we can follow, from the dates and headings of those faded old pages, his slow path, climbing steadily to the northeast.

The first letter was from Cincinnati, dated March 18. Since the town was so near Huntsville, it's possible he would have either traveled on horseback or been taken in a buggy to catch the stage from there, probably early the next morning. He obviously wrote this one late at night: "I hope you are at this moment, blest with sweet repose, and pray that you will awake in the morning refreshed, & cheerful." Then he warned her that she would hear of "some slanders against me" recently reported in a Galveston newspaper, concerning alleged misappropriation of the republic's funds for his personal use when he had been president. "I have not seen the piece, but will soon. All that I wish is for you to be assured, whatever, is false & slanderous!" Then he let a comment his young son had recently voiced about something or other echo his assurance that all would be well. "As Sam [Jr.] said, 'Pa will fix it!!!'"[1]

The next installment came from Sabine Town, on the Texas-Louisiana border, dated four days later. He recounted that he had ridden that day for several hours in an uncovered stage during a driving rainstorm pushed by a "cold Norther." Finally, he got to wherever he would spend the night and found "a pretty good fire." He was, no doubt, writing the letter beside it.

Plotting out the rest of his journey, he said he felt "much disposed, to go by way of Tennessee" to visit "Sister Wallace," his younger sibling Mary Houston Wallace, called Polly by the family, who had suffered a mental breakdown, not her first, and was currently institutionalized in Knoxville. "I hope it [his visit] may have some effect on her mind, for the better. Should it be so, I will feel more happy than I cou'd be, were I in possession of all the wealth of California."[2] That soon-to-be state with its abundance of newly discovered gold was surely much on his mind during his journey, for its admittance as a slave-free state was currently the contentious subject of the compromise debates.

Polly had been emotionally delicate for years. In 1829 Houston's letters from his drunken exile with the Cherokees after his first, failed marriage had been kept from her lest they put her over the edge. When her husband, Matthew Wallace, died, she soon married his brother, General William Wallace. It's possible that second union was a disastrous one,[3] which might have pushed her beyond her breaking point and landed her in the a mental asylum. But Houston, never shy of making diagnoses he wasn't qualified to make, blamed her plight on a trio of causes: menopause, a brain abscess (where he came up with that one is anyone's guess), and, most troubling to him of all, their sister Eliza's harsh and relentless reproaches about her remarriage.[4]

The whole business had long caused ongoing turmoil in the family and was especially troubling to Houston, who felt a special fondness for Polly and obviously considered her his favorite sibling. "Her situation is a cause of great sorrow to me," he confided to Margaret in the letter written by that much-appreciated fire, "& the cause of it, (as I believe,) adds poignantly, to my grief." It was nearly midnight when he was ready to put pen and ink away, and the stage had not yet arrived that would take him farther along his trek the next day. "If it does not [arrive] I will get a horse, and go on tomorrow, or next day, if I live."[5] The last phrase was one commonly used in that era when practically any ailment could turn deadly, when even a slight infection, and certainly a case of influenza or pneumonia, might very well mean the end. And having spent much of the day in a driving, cold rainstorm would have put him at particular risk. In 1850 when writers bid "good-bye"—the snipped-off remnant of the original and more beautiful "God be with you"—to someone they weren't likely to see for a while, it might have been not only a blessing but a final farewell.

The stagecoach didn't show up quickly enough for him, so he did hire or purchase a horse—it was apparently a common practice to buy a mount in full confidence that it could be sold to a livery stable at the destination—and rode it to Grand Ecore, halfway across Louisiana, and the next day, over the remainder of the state to where the Red River flows into the Mississippi. While waiting there, on March 26, for a paddle-wheeler to take him up to Nashville, he sent Margaret some instructions.

"While I think of it my Love," he wrote, "if Col. Long, of Crockett [a town near Huntsville named for possibly the most famous of the Alamo's fallen heroes], calls upon, or sends to you, for two pigs of the white sow, give, or send them to him." Then he remembered to give her some news about a baby born to a couple they knew in Sabine Town. "A nine pounder," he reported, apparently as impressed with the size of the child as he would be with that of a fish pulled from a lake. The couple's other children were, he reminded her, "monsters for size" and their daughter "quite pretty, but I don't like her beauty as much, as I do that of our 'gals.' Indeed, I see none that I do admire, so much as them."[6]

On the same day that he was writing that note, Margaret was in the process of sending some sad news to him, which he wouldn't read until several days after his arrival in Washington. His sister Eliza, the apparent persecutor of Polly, had died nearly a week before somewhere near Huntsville. The news must have come late to Margaret: "I did not know that your sister was ill, until I heard that she was no more. She died very suddenly, and from what I can learn, her disease must have been an inflammation of the brain." Medical records listed the cause of Eliza Houston Moore's death as "apoplexy,"[7] now usually called a stroke. She also reported that a bad hailstorm had blown through during the previous night, full of thunder and lightning, and that she, after a "desolation of spirit" due to his departure, was doing better and that her cough was much improved. "I am alive," she declared, "and a wonder to myself."[8]

The third day of April found Houston safely delivered upriver to Nashville. Two days later he sent Margaret a description of his voyage: "The cholera was much in Orleans. The river was all over its banks." After mentioning a brief stop in Memphis to visit some "kindred," he closed with more instructions: "Today I send you a Hogshead [barrel] of bacon, hams, sides, shoulders, & it will be sent to Rice and Nichols, Houston. Get Gibbs to have all our hauling done."[9]

Why he would be transporting pork from Tennessee to Texas when there were hogs in his own pen, two of which he had recently sold or given away, is not clear. But he had a tendency to do things on the spur of the moment, availing himself of life's little offerings when they presented themselves. Margaret was probably never surprised at whatever showed up at her doorstep.

The next dispatch, dated "6th Apl," came from Sparta, a hundred or so miles east of Nashville, where he called on some acquaintances named

Donelson, who proudly showed him their six-week-old daughter whom he thought "clever and pretty, I think, as young babys [*sic*] are." Surely thinking of the imminent Houston arrival, he shared a bit about how the infant was outfitted: "I was pleased with the way their baby was fixed, and I requested a pattern of it from Mrs. D, which she gave me, and directions how to have it made." He promised to have it made up when he reached Washington and to mail it to her. "It is German, and the baby is lain upon it like placing it on a pillow, only it is in a dress, as well as an arm couch. I am sure you will be delighted with it, and amused at it." He mentioned that a cousin had recently told him, probably in Memphis, that he had heard that his sister Polly was improving; Houston was obviously apprehensive about his upcoming visit with her. Then he told Margaret he would be sending along some good apple seeds that should be soaked for twelve hours before being planted. He ended with this: "Dearest! I would rather than the state of Tennessee, that I could be with you, and remain so, while we live on earth."[10]

• • •

Houston finally saw his sister Polly a few days later. He described the encounter in a letter dashed off hurriedly in Blountsville, Tennessee, on the thirteenth, during a brief middle-of-the-night layover at a stage depot. "She knew me, and was very glad to see me," he wrote, assuring Margaret that she had sent her love to her and the children and that she had promised to write to her. "She thinks so, but she will not unless she should improve."[11]

Though he allowed that Polly was treated with all the kindness that "her situation will permit," one can only imagine what an institution for the mentally ill would have been like in the mid-nineteenth century. It would not have been an attractive place, and certainly not a cheerful one, where patients were hardly expected to get better, and before the discovery of any medicines or therapies to help them do so. The attendants would have been on their best behavior with a family member visiting, especially one who was a national celebrity.

"She embraced me just as she had always done," he wrote. "For hours in general conversation, she was as rational, and her style, and language, as good as ever. You would suppose that it could not be possible,"—one of his multitudinous commas pops up here, probably actually needed for once, since he surely would have paused before finishing his thought—"that she was insane." He noted that she had not been confined in her room for "a long time." In fact, their visit took place in a common parlor, where she refused to sit in a chair but seemed comfortable on the floor. "They have great trouble to keep shoes, & stockings on her," he wrote, "and she will not wear anything on her head." During their meal she consented to sit in a chair at the table but refused to eat. Instead she talked, telling stories about Houston as a boy, one of them about him stealing cream from the spring house.

"She never smiles," he continued, "but looks pleasant, but never cheerful. . . . She never uses any expression, in company that is improper, but is perfectly delicate, in every thing." The sad state he found her in must have rekindled his displeasure and disappointment with their sister Eliza, whose cruel treatment of Polly was, he believed, at least partly to blame for her madness. "She [Polly] is now a wreck of a noble mind," he concluded, "and the most foully, & cruelly slandered female, on earth, in my opinion." Written at midnight in the little depot, Houston's letter ends with his appraisal of a landscape that matched his mood. "This country looks dreary. The oaks have not yet cast their old leaves, and there is, but little appearance of verdure."[12]

He had much to ponder when he crawled up into the stage in the wee hours of the cold morning to cross the border into Virginia. As a clopping team of horses pulled him along muddy roads through the damp, dark night, Houston, whether he closed his eyes and tried to sleep or watched for occasional cabin windows flickering with pale candlelight, must have worked his way through the little litany of woes that plagued him mightily: Margaret, ill and troubled at home without him beside her when she very much needed him to be; one sister wasting away in a shadowy half existence partly caused by the mistreatment of another; the federal Union that held his heart and his total allegiance grasping at straws to stay together. And there was the new baby due to make an entrance at any time, the one that Margaret was most worried about. The first three had arrived hale and hearty, screaming and full of life, a rich blessing in itself in a time when there were many awfully tiny coffins buried in churchyards. This time he must have wondered how far their good fortune would stretch.

To add insult to injury, the section of Virginia he always most enjoyed traveling through, where he had been born and spent his first thirteen years, offered him what he would later call "a cool reception for a son of the Old Dominion." There was a snowstorm in Rockbridge County during his transit.[13] If any of his extensive reading—he no doubt had a few worn volumes in his satchel for the long days of travel—had taken him into Shakespeare, a line from *Hamlet* might have come to mind on that dreary last leg of his long voyage: "When sorrows come they come not single spies," King Claudius muses in the fourth act, "but in battalions."[14] Houston would not put pen to paper again until he was in back in Washington.

• • •

Two days after he posted that last letter from Blountsville, his friend Henderson Yoakum scribbled out a short note to the senator while in Livingston, the county seat of Polk County, some forty miles from Huntsville. Yoakum, a lawyer, had a case there. "Being here at court," he wrote, "I recd. a note from home yesterday giving the news that you had another daughter. You will doubtless have heard it ere this."[15] The baby had arrived on April 9, healthy, robust, and with enough hair for her mother to snip a bit of it to mail to her father.

Ten

Back in Washington Houston, none the worse for wear except for a bad cold,[1] put his worries aside as best he could and focused on the all-important business at hand, especially that part of it relative to Texas. During his absence the Senate had been a hotbed of activity, working its way feverishly through the impassioned debates over the propositions Henry Clay had intricately pieced together for his massive omnibus bill.

If it eventually passed later in the session, its overall effect would be staggering. California would be admitted as a slave-free state, and the territories of New Mexico and Utah, a wide expanse comprising what would eventually be five western states, would be given the right to make up their own minds regarding slavery, an act of manifest destiny, an old concept with a new name. The sprawling state boundaries that Texas claimed to be those of the old republic would be significantly reduced in exchange for ten million dollars paid by the Union to erase the debt incurred during Texas' war with Mexico, provided the state legislature approve the sale of roughly one-third of its land to the federal government in what would amount to a mammoth real estate transaction. A fugitive slave law, making it illegal for anyone to harbor runaway slaves, would be enacted (as a concession to the South), and a prohibition of the buying and selling of slaves—though not the possession of them—would be imposed in the District of Columbia (as a concession to the North).[2]

In short, it would reconfigure the nation, solidify the institution of slavery in some of its parts while negating it in others, and hopefully serve as enough of a hodgepodge of pacification to mollify the factions threatening to rip the Union apart. Houston, nurtured almost from his boyhood on the rich milk of Jacksonian democracy—Union first, foremost and forever—was a loud, colorful (donned in the Indian blankets and wide sombreros he often showed up in), and adamant champion of the bill, setting himself apart from his colleagues from the South.

Since his arrival in the Senate in 1846 his focus had progressively become more strongly centered on national affairs than on regional needs, causing his popularity to rise in the Northeast and fall off in the

South, especially in the state he represented. While his agenda was, in theory at least, what the Founding Fathers must have intended for the legislative branch of government—its upper house seeing to the nation as a whole; the lower, to its individual states' concerns—it had never managed to quite work that way. Senators and representatives alike fought and schemed regularly to bring home the goods (which would not be called "pork" for another couple of decades) in federal contracts, new military posts, and sundry other appealing windfalls to the constituents in their home states whose gratitude, they hoped, would translate into enough votes to keep them in office.

Much of the debate over California, New Mexico, and Utah focused on the Wilmot Proviso, a piece of failed legislation, reproposed on a regular basis, that would ban slavery in any territory acquired in the Mexican-American War.[3] First introduced by Pennsylvania representative David Wilmot in 1846 as a codicil to an appropriations bill intended to pay for the war, the proviso had been passed by the House but killed in the Senate, which was its fate again the following year. Now it was being dredged up yet again by anti-slavery congressmen who scrambled for any means available to further their agenda.

The compromise bill, if passed, would finally plunge a stake through the Wilmot Proviso since the issue of slavery in all former Mexican lands would be settled. California would enter the Union as a free state, and the New Mexico and Utah Territories would be given the eventual freedom to make their own decisions. Texas had won its independence from Mexico at San Jacinto and was later admitted as a slave state of its own volition, thus igniting the war that had given birth to the proviso in the first place.

Even with the proviso dead and buried, Henry Clay's carefully formulated attempt to provide a thread to keep the Union patched together, however precariously, seemed more and more to be a wasted, unattainable possibility. In order for it to have any chance of success, a bit of deus ex machina would have to emerge, something totally unpredicted and unexpected that might bridge a gaping abyss in the Senate that had grown about as wide as it could possibly get.

An ever-increasing number of southerners like Calhoun and company, touting secession as their only viable path, were gearing up for a convention in Nashville where they intended to chart what seemed to be their obvious course. And many of their anti-slavery northern colleagues—

their passions constantly fueled in print and from town hall meetings and church pulpits by men like William Lloyd Garrison, the editor of the *Liberator*, and Wendell Phillips, a fiery abolitionist lawyer and public speaker—saw the South's eventual departure as the sole means of conveniently sweeping slavery out of the nation forever.[4]

And then a glimmer of hope flickered in the growing darkness. In early March—while Houston was in Huntsville—Senator Daniel Webster of Massachusetts rose to his feet and provided what would, more than any previous attempt, finally nudge the adoption of Clay's resolutions into the realm of possibility.[5] But it would come at a great personal price. Webster, the son of a New England farmer and a graduate of Phillips Exeter Academy and Dartmouth College, had served eight years in the House of Representatives, nearly twenty more in the Senate, and had been secretary of state in the Harrison and Tyler administrations. He had made three unsuccessful bids for the presidency. And with this address, which would be forever after known as simply the Seventh of March Speech, he would effectively scuttle any aspirations he might still harbor for a fourth attempt.[6]

He set the tone with an opening salvo that has since been chiseled into history: "Mr. Speaker," he said, his tall, gaunt body ramrod straight in his customary black tailcoat and wide cravat, "I wish to speak today, not as a Massachusetts man, or as a Northern man, but as an American, and as a member of the Senate of the United States."[7] Thus, the olive branch of unity and compromise was immediately tossed into the chamber that represented every senator's common bond. And this from a man who had never been anything of a compromiser, neither in 1820 when Clay paved the way for the Missouri provisions nor in 1833 when South Carolina's Ordinance of Nullification had been hushed by careful conciliation. Throughout his long and brilliant career he had consistently and aggressively aligned himself with those opposed to slavery, a formidable bloc that surely expected him to stay as true to that narrow road in this address as he had in countless others.

He spoke for three hours, during which time he never, according to a dispatch in the following day's New York *Daily Times* by S. P. Lyman, "looked at his notes except to take from them extracts which he asked Mr. Greene of Rhode Island, whose seat is near his own, to read for him. He never transposed a sentence, or attempted to change the phraseology of an idea he had put forth; but the speech came on, as the Mississippi rolls from its fountains, increasing in depth and width till it terminates in the ocean."[8]

Aside from the fact that the Mississippi rolls into a gulf rather than an ocean, Lyman's appraisal was probably spot on. Webster had long had a reputation as both an adept navigator through thorny issues and a gifted orator. He would, a bit more than a century later, be named by a Senate committee chaired by a young freshman lawmaker named John F. Kennedy as one of the five greatest senators in American history, a short list that also included Clay and Calhoun.[9]

The day, according to Lyman's account in the *Daily Times*, was "glorious," with every square foot of the room except for the senators' chairs filled with guests clutching official passes. The lobby was packed with an overflow crowd interspersed with members of the House of Representatives who had walked down the hall to witness what they suspected would be a momentous event. "There was not," Lyman wrote, "unoccupied a spot in that chamber, above or below, or in any avenue leading to it, where the sound of Mr. Webster's voice could be heard."[10] And that vast crowd heard something very different from the venerable New Englander than anyone expected.

As the afternoon wore on, Webster found, as expected, much to celebrate in the Union but also much to criticize in its two polarized sections currently at odds, finding equal fault in the northern abolitionists who had heretofore been his staunch allies and in the southern faction intent on war. Regarding the rumored upcoming convention to discuss secession to be held in Nashville, he warned its intended participants that "if they meet for any purpose hostile to the Union, they have been singularly inappropriate in their selection of a place," going on to remind them that anyone contriving in that city to overthrow the Union would do so "over the bones of Andrew Jackson."

At the end of it, when the assembled audience must have ached to stand and stretch and when Webster himself, at sixty-eight, had to have longed to be done and fall back into his seat, he issued a last clear challenge to his brethren. "Instead of speaking of the possibility or utility of secession," he said, his voice somehow as full of passion and strength as it had been at the outset, "instead of dwelling in those caverns of darkness; instead of groping with those ideas so full of all that is horrid and horrible, let us come into the light of day; let us enjoy the fresh air of Liberty and Union."

Then, having sailed the course of compromise that he must have realized would move him irrevocably beyond any further abolitionist support, he concluded: "Let us raise our conceptions to the magnitude and the importance of the duties that dissolve upon us; let our comprehension be as broad as the county for which we act, our aspirations as high as its certain destiny; let us not be pigmies in a case that calls for men."[11]

By the time Sam Houston returned to his Senate desk, the informal consensus was that, because of Webster's unexpected support of the legislation and his impassioned appeal for considerable concessions from both extremes, Clay's bill stood a better than average chance of passing. But everyone realized that the old Yankee had fallen on his sword to purchase it. Proof of it came quickly, in scathing editorials and considerable backroom chatter, and in speeches by and letters from colleagues of long standing who now publicly distanced themselves from him.

One repudiation even came in verse. The renowned Quaker poet John Greenleaf Whittier, an ardent abolitionist whose most anthologized offering, "Snowbound," would torment schoolchildren for more than a century, published a poem that was obviously about Webster, a Massachusetts neighbor. His greatest disappointment with Webster's support of the omnibus bill was that the old abolitionist could tolerate the section that would create a fugitive slave act, requiring citizens living in the North to return runaway slaves to their owners in the South.[12] He titled the poem "Ichabod," which translated from Hebrew means "the glory is departed."

So fallen! So lost! The light withdrawn
Which once he wore!
The glory from his gray hairs gone
Forevermore!

There were six more stanzas that cast the old senator even deeper into the mire of disrepute and oblivion before the poet twisted the knife forcibly.

. . . from those great eyes
The soul has fled.
When faith is lost, when honor dies,

The man is dead!
Then, pay the reverence of old days
To his dead fame;
Walk backward, with averted gaze,
And hide the shame![13]

Daniel Webster concluded his long and historic service to the Union he loved by beginning one more term as secretary of state, in the Fillmore administration, before falling ill and passing into history himself. His legacy is preserved in that history, and more tangibly in numerous busts and statues throughout New England, his stern, chiseled visage staring out through deluges of autumn leaves and winter snowfalls, and in the old House of Representatives chamber, now called Statuary Hall, in the US Capitol. He also lives on in a piece of literature that fared considerably better than the vindictive poem penned by Whittier.

In "The Devil and Daniel Webster," a short story written by Stephen Vincent Benet between the world wars in the next century that would be for many years assigned as something of a rite of passage to American junior high school students, Webster is called on to defend an unlucky New Hampshire farmer named Jabez Stone, who has foolishly sold his soul to Satan in exchange for better crops and more prosperity. Webster's defense is that an American citizen may not be forced into the service of a foreign prince.

The wily devil, known as "Old Scratch" in those parts, contends that he is no foreigner but an American himself. "When the first wrong was done to the first Indian," he maintains, "I was there. When the first slaver put out for the Congo, I stood on her deck."[14] He even consents to try the case before an American jury, filling it with notorious scoundrels and traitors to tilt the odds in his favor. Not deterred, Webster appeals to the infamous jurors' contributions, though disreputable, in building the Union and in what he knows must—they being souls cast forever into the devil's awful domain—be their strong hunger for freedom. The jury finds for Jabez, of course, and Satan moves on to fight other battles.

At the beginning of the story, which is written as an old folk tale told down generations, the narrator says of Daniel Webster, "Every time there's a thunderstorm around Marshfield [Webster's hometown], they say you can hear his rolling voice in the hollows of the sky. And they say that if you go to his grave and speak loud and clear 'Dan'l Webster—Dan'l Webster!' the ground'll begin to shiver and the trees begin to shake. And after a while you'll hear a deep voice saying, 'Neighbor, how stands the Union?' Then you better answer the Union stands as she stood, rock-bottomed and copper sheathed, one and indivisible, or he's liable to rear right out of the ground."[15]

It's a work of fiction, obviously. But Webster's zealous devotion to his country staying united is no exaggeration. The fact that he knowingly, in a single speech, put forever out of reach his longest-held personal ambition in an attempt to preserve it is proof positive.

Though Sam Houston's Senate seat was empty that afternoon, he would know the text of the address soon enough. One must wonder if he had a little glimpse, reading the words that sealed Webster's sacrifice, of his own future.

• • •

Less than a month later, on the last day of March, John C. Calhoun died of tuberculosis at the age of sixty-eight. Thomas Rusk, who came considerably closer to sharing the old firebrand's ideology than his fellow Texas senator, delivered a moving tribute on the floor of the Senate. Rusk had known Calhoun since his boyhood in South Carolina; Calhoun had been a neighbor of the Rusk family and had secured young Thomas his first political appointment in the district clerk's office so he could earn his living while studying law.[16]

It's highly doubtful that Sam Houston—who was still bouncing, floating, and galloping his way toward Washington—would have risen to say anything about Calhoun even if he had been present. He was, if anything, a master at holding grudges. Once back in the capital city, Houston spent his days in the Senate chamber scratching out notes for upcoming speeches, whittling constantly away at bits of soft pine with his pocketknife, casting votes whenever the roll was called, and sometimes actually paying attention as a colleague rambled on through a motion or an address.

When one of the Senate pages, boys of about twelve or thirteen who were orphans or sons of widowed mothers in need of some extra income, brought the mail to his desk, Houston would thumb through the stack of folded missives—mostly requests for assistance in seeking some government appointment or another; it seemed that practically every man with a patch to plow and a tax to pay in Texas wanted to be a postmaster—looking for letters from Margaret. These he would open first, often spilling several dried wildflowers from his children on his desk.

He attended meetings of senators, though fewer than he once had. He found the reception cool and pointedly reserved at Democratic Party gatherings because of his support of Clay's bill, and neither, of course, was he welcome in councils of the Whigs, though his current mind-set was much more in alignment with theirs. He also curtailed almost all of his social life, possibly because of Margaret's occasional cautions about the perils of gadding about, like a peacock, at balls and teas. That "praise of man is an empty thing" comment in one of her letters from a couple of years before had likely stung.

So his evenings were spent in his rented room reading and writing to friends and supporters, but most often to Margaret. When he learned of the arrival of his third daughter, Mary William, he expressed his delight at the news and added that Sam Jr. would "feel the apparent injustice" in being deprived of the little brother he wanted and having to make do, so far, with a batch of sisters.[17]

On Sundays he went to church, at first because he knew that Margaret wanted him to but finally because he grew to like the pastor. When first shaking the hand of Reverend George Whitfield Samson on the front steps of the E. Street Baptist Church, Houston, wearing a multicolored Indian blanket as a cape, confessed that he would not have ordinarily been in attendance but for his wife, "one of the best Christians on earth."[18] Every week thereafter he sat in his favorite pew, took out his knife and whittled, and listened carefully to Samson's sermons, usually discussing them later with the minister who soon became a close friend, sometimes praising the topic or delivery and as often challenging his interpretation of scripture.

But he, to Margaret's continual regret, still refused to be baptized. Undeterred, she continued to hold out hope. In one of her frequent letters she warned him that "you have nothing but the great world about you, with its heartlessness and mockery of joy." But she went on to say that she was "enjoying the sweet belief" that he would eventually "draw from the word of God, from prayer and meditation, rich consolation."[19] Time would tell, but so far Sam Houston's spirituality seemed to consist of whittling away during Sunday-morning sermons and then arguing about them with the preacher.

• • •

The much-heralded Nashville convention to consider the South's secession from the Union convened on June 3, with only nine states represented. And more than a few of the delegates from those states came with what one historian would later call "dubious credentials."[20] Without Calhoun's thunder the convention lost much of its steam, and it ended up accomplishing little more than sending some of the more disappointed attendees home to make loud, self-serving speeches about what might have been. Two of them, Henderson and Wigfall, were from Texas.[21]

The omnibus bill that had taken up the lion's share of the Senate's time and energy failed to pass on the last day of July. Senator Clay wasted no time in announcing that its various parts would be revamped, introduced as individual bills, and sent forth to fare on their own. President Taylor had died less than a month before, and the new president, Millard Fillmore, was much more receptive to the various sections of the bill than his predecessor had been. That, and the fact that the South's most vocal mouthpiece, Calhoun, was dead, gave Clay hope that his long, hard efforts could finally reach fruition. But those efforts, coupled with his rapidly declining health—like Calhoun, Clay suffered from tuberculosis—had taken their toll, and he was too ill to wage the battle any further. He handed the job of shepherding the bills through the Senate to Stephen A. Douglas of Illinois.

Aided by an outbreak of armed conflict between the Mexican army and federal forces on the Mexican border—nothing so unifies the bickering factions of a democracy as foreign aggression against its common cause—each of the bills passed in September. So the long, contentious session that had seemed would never come to an end finally did. Calhoun was dead. Clay was dying. Webster's hopes for the presidency were dashed. And Sam Houston went home.

Eleven

In Huntsville Margaret had spent the spring slowly regaining her stamina after the difficult birth of her fourth child and the welcomed departure of Virginia Thorne with the former overseer Thomas Gott. Given that her usually robust mobility had been considerably curtailed—precluding visits into town to Gibbs and other merchants and maybe even to church, though it's difficult to imagine anything short of being on her deathbed keeping her away from church—each of her days must have been a precise imitation of the last one and a predictable harbinger of the next.

She would have read a good deal and regularly dipped the sharp nib of her pen into ink to maintain constant correspondence with family and friends in distant places. But most of her multipage letters were addressed to her husband. In early May she wrote to Houston that she had "had a long and wearisome confinement and although the baby is five weeks old today, I am just able to walk about my room. I have not exposed myself at all, but it seems impossible for me to recover my strength."[1] She might have sat in a rocker and watched the children playing in the yard, periodically glancing up the road that ran beside her front gate for any friends, Baptist ladies all, that might come down in their buggies from town to call.

In spite of Margaret's natural shyness and introversion, her home was, because of her standing in her church and the town but mostly because of her famous husband, one of the social epicenters in Huntsville.[2] During Houston's sojourns from Washington elaborate dinners were regularly carried in from Eliza's freestanding kitchen and served to numerous guests on makeshift tables set up in the parlor or, if the weather permitted, in the dogtrot hallway or out on the lawn.

Blue and white tureens and platters, their purchases all recorded in the Gibbs Brothers' ledgers, sat with wide china plates and silver cutlery on damask tablecloths that had made the trip a decade before from Alabama. Fresh-cut flowers from the beds out front, arranged in pottery vases, would have provided the centerpieces in spring and summer, perhaps pansies or sprigs of holly in winter. A monogrammed bowl, filled either with a festive punch or yuletide eggnog—both sans bourbon or rum—had been a gift from the sultan of Morocco when Houston was president of the Republic of Texas. If chairs were scarce, Sam Jr. would perch on a mahogany medicine chest his father had requisitioned, probably quite unofficially, from the defeated general Santa Anna at San Jacinto.[3]

In addition to townsfolk, traveling preachers would show up regularly. And anyone, from anywhere in the nation, with a letter of introduction to Houston could expect a good meal and lively conversation, even if whatever position or appointment he had come for came to naught. Political allies would pull up to the table before talking strategy later with their host, always out in his office away from Margaret's hearing.

All in all, the Houstons opened the doors to their home and their abundant table as willingly as Geoffrey Chaucer's Franklin, the generous landowner in his *Canterbury Tales*. The difference was, however, that the Franklin was wealthy and could afford to do it. The Houstons could not. But frugal as Margaret tried to be, her husband never seemed to fret about money or to care much one way or another about it. He was as often in debt as he was solvent, and his accounts rarely showed much, if anything, in the way of savings. Perfectly adept at serving as a steward of public funds—especially during his second stint as president of the republic, when he attempted to shore up the economy after inheriting depleted coffers from his predecessor, Mirabeau Lamar, and then as a senator when negotiating the sale of Texas lands to the federal government in the Compromise of 1850—he was unsuccessful, and seemingly uninterested, in balancing his household budget.[4]

When something was needed for his wife, his children, his slaves, or the homestead, he somehow managed to provide it. And when visitors came calling, they were fed. When Houston was away, which was most of the time, the gatherings in Margaret's parlor were less frequent and significantly smaller. He was the enticing beacon, his the voice that filled the rooms and the gravity that established the orbits of those standing in them. Margaret was perfectly content blending in with the crowd, happiest at the fringe while her husband held court.

An intimate tea or light meal with one or several friends was much more to her liking than big festivities with too much loud chatter. It was probably at one of those little soirées that she learned that Virginia Thorne had returned to Huntsville to go to school—apparently she and Melinda

Rankin had parted ways in nearby Cincinnati—and was staying with a family named Wilson, acquaintances of the Houstons.

Before long some gossip started working its way through town about Margaret having mistreated Virginia in some way before she ran off with Gott, and that Benjamin Wilson believed it to be true. Margaret had toyed with the idea, the year before, of taking the matter of Virginia's relationship with Gott, when it had first begun, before the Baptist Church to help her determine how to best deal with it. But her friends had advised against it, calling the involvement of the church her final option. Keep such business in your own household, they suggested.[5]

The problem now was that Virginia was no longer *in* her household. And though that very fact had initially seemed to provide the answer to Margaret's prayers, the perfect solution to the problem, the girl had ended up in a household that seemed inclined to pay serious attention to her grumbling and whatever tales she might be telling.

In a letter to Houston dated May 21 Margaret wrote that she suspected that Benjamin Wilson had been the "grand instigator of the whole plot, but God forbid that I should judge too harshly." She added that the town was abuzz with the rumor—"the world is busy with the affair" as she put it, her world being much smaller than her husband's—and that she intended to stay secluded in her "quiet home" and "try to look calmly on the storm as it passes by."[6] This is exactly what she seems to have done.

As she got stronger, she ventured forth on pleasant days with the children out into the nearest meadow where they picked wildflowers. At night she read them Bible stories and led them in their prayers before tucking them into their beds.[7] When her mother was in residence, she—not likely to have missed out on any reading of scripture or any opportunity to interject her puritanical interpretation of it—would slowly and heavily ascend the steep steps, sending a shiver through the skeleton of the house.

The baby, Mary Willie (called Mollie by the family), slept in a crib beside Margaret's bed downstairs. Eliza, during the convalescence of her mistress, probably spent as much time in the house as in her little log cabin kitchen or her section of the slave quarters, tending to the needs of the baby and the trio of other little Houstons that Margaret would normally see to. She was totally devoted to her, having been her dependable companion since they had both been little girls in Alabama. The children called her Aunt Eliza.

Rain drifted in sporadically as spring slid into summer, in sudden deluges full of thunder and lightning at times and sometimes tapping lightly on the window as Margaret rocked the newest addition to the family or read in the evenings. It was a pleasant time of recuperation and domestic happiness, made even sweeter by the knowledge that she was getting better and that her husband would be home soon. Then, in early summer, the storm that she had resolved to watch as it passed by landed soundly on her doorstep.

• • •

It took no time at all for Huntsville's citizens to learn that the Houston's former overseer Thomas Gott had gotten himself appointed as Virginia Thorne's guardian.[8] The girl had originally told Gott, then past his mid-twenties, that she was nineteen. So when he learned that she was actually only fourteen, he must have figured the guardianship scenario would play better than a romance. In his new capacity he had gone to the courthouse and filed charges on Virginia's behalf against Margaret for assault and battery.[9]

The previous December there had been an incident involving Margaret, Virginia, and one of the children, the specifics of which are muddled by two differing recollections. Apparently Margaret and Virginia had been upstairs getting the children into bed for the night. Four-year-old Nannie wouldn't go to sleep, so Margaret told Virginia to get her out of bed. Obviously agitated that she had just been told to put her *into* the bed, she jerked the child up and brusquely plopped her onto the floor. Nannie started wailing, and Margaret accused Virginia of having hurt her. Virginia, spitting out her response in her typical acidic delivery, said, "I am *not* hurting it," employing what was probably not the wisest choice of pronouns in the presence of a loving mother who was already angry.[10]

At that point is where the two accounts diverge. After the incident Virginia told Gott, by then her sole confidant and perhaps her sweetheart, that Margaret had refused to listen to her explanation and knocked her against a bedpost and proceeded to thrash her soundly twenty or so times with a cowhide whip on her back and arms.[11] Margaret would later admit to having let her sudden anger get the best of her and pushing the girl, but she apparently never owned up to the whipping, or at least not to one of that magnitude.

In all likelihood the actual events probably fell somewhere between the two conflicting stories; Margaret likely did strike Virginia, but how a cowhide whip would have come so readily to hand in a little girl's bedroom is perplexing. In any event, the charges were entered into one of the big ledgers in the clerk of the court's office, and Margaret was summoned to appear for a preliminary hearing, where a trial date was set for September 30.

Houston, still embroiled with the compromise bill debates in the Senate, wouldn't be able to be present for the proceedings, so he wrote to his friend and fellow lawyer Henderson Yoakum, asking him to serve as counsel for the defense. Yoakum suspected that the entire business was a case of purely political shenanigans aimed at harming Margaret's husband.[12] Sam Houston had absolutely no doubt of it.

As early as 1846, four years previously, he had told Margaret in one of his first letters from Washington that "the object of my enemies now will be to assail me in domestic relations. They know that they [his family] are dearer to me than any other thing on earth! The assaults will be, I apprehend, against the females of my family. This they think would render me desperate, and thereby, they would gain the only advantage which they now hope to obtain."[13]

He and Yoakum were convinced that someone or several people—political enemies, constituents who hadn't received the preferential treatment or specific legislation they wanted, or just a group angry at where their senator stood on certain issues—were intent on doing harm to Houston's reputation by besmirching his wife's and had somehow enlisted the conveniently placed Gott to bring the charges. Yoakum, deep into the research and writing of his history of Texas and involved in important issues at Austin College where he, like Houston, was a member of the board, retained A. P. Wiley, another Huntsville lawyer, to assist him.

Margaret's friends rallied around her. Even Jane Wilson, who had brought Virginia into her home and whose husband had, in all likelihood, been part and parcel to the accusation and prosecution, showed up to offer comfort, though perhaps of the somewhat cold variety. Houston's advice to Margaret, in letters written at his Senate desk or in his rented Washington room, was simplicity itself: rise above the turmoil and pay no attention to it. This was hard medicine to swallow, of course, in her little town and little life and not accustomed to the constant barrage of denigration that her husband faced and rebuffed—"like water off a duck's back" he often said—on a daily basis.

But beyond her friends' comfort and her husband's support Margaret, to no one's surprise who knew her, put her complete confidence in the hands of divine providence. That, she figured, would have to do.

Twelve

Margaret's trial was eventually called to order in the new courthouse on the public square in Huntsville. Virginia took the stand first and gave her recollection of the alleged assault and the events that led up to it. Lawyers' attempts to establish her age were confused by her testimony that she had no idea how old she was. She went on to admit that she hadn't even known about the current proceedings until a couple of days before, adding that Gott and some other men had organized everything. She displayed some scars on her elbow and wrist that she claimed to be from Margaret's beating, still visible long after they would have been inflicted.[1]

Margaret's brother Vernal Lea testified that as far as he knew, he was still the girl's legal guardian, recounting how he and his late wife had taken on that responsibility several years previously in Galveston when Virginia had been seven. This meant she would have been fourteen when she ran off with Gott. In what was clearly an understatement Lea allowed that Virginia had proven early on to be "hard to manage."[2]

Finally, several people were sworn in and attested to Margaret's sterling character and good works, but she did not take the stand herself. The jury was sent out to consider their verdict and after a while informed the judge they couldn't reach a decision. Perhaps looking at his watch and wanting his dinner, he made a decision of his own that seems almost unbelievable in modern times, but perhaps not so in a small town in the middle of the nineteenth century. He referred the case to the Baptist church, which promptly found Margaret not guilty.[3]

Whatever Margaret felt about the hung jury she never recorded. But following the scriptural dictate to render unto Caesar what is Caesar's and unto God what is God's, she would have welcomed her vindication in what she surely considered the higher court.

• • •

Houston arrived in Huntsville in the late fall, having fled Washington after the various sections of the original compromise bill had been passed. At home, however, there was a bit more work to do. Because the Texas component depended on the sale of a massive tract of its land to the Union, the state legislature had to approve the transaction. The federal government could tease and tamper with the nation's boundaries, as it had done with the Oregon Territory and the border between Louisiana and the Republic of Texas during the Mexican-American War, but individual state's borders were sacrosanct and couldn't be redrawn without the state's consent.

Houston immediately took to the stump, urging ratification. He made numerous speeches at county courthouses, in Austin, and in the shade of convenient trees. Some in the various crowds, seeing the old hero of San Jacinto, flocked around to shake his hand and sing his praises. Others, a growing number of others, seeing the misguided senator who had fallen in with northerners opposed to slavery and dedicated to a Union that Houston himself had shoved Texas into, and one they currently distrusted, either jeered him or stayed away altogether.

• • •

The year 1850, which had been so very loud in so many ways, finally drew quietly toward its conclusion. Home for a while, Houston introduced himself to Mary Willie, the newest member of the family, and spent much of his time with Sam Jr., Nannie, and Maggie—and with Margaret, of course. He brushed the whole Virginia Thorne episode off as pure political dirty trickery and encouraged his wife to do the same.

They attended church for Sunday-morning services and for various prayer meetings, Mary Willie held by one of them, Nancy Lea—if she was there at the time—and the three older children arranged like descending stairsteps beside them, the whole contingent filling up a pew.

Autumn sent russet leaves fluttering through gray days, swooshing them off to other places. Then the first hard freezes of winter fell heavy on Margaret's flower beds and fruit trees and Eliza's garden. The two redbrick chimneys, sturdy bookends at either end of the house, sent out constant wood smoke into cold, blustery days.

Christmas was a quiet affair at Woodland with an empty chair at the head of the table, for Houston had already left to return to Washington. A yuletide tree might have been chosen by the children and chopped down by Joshua somewhere on the property. The tradition of decorating trees, begun in the ancient Roman feast of Saturnalia, had been recently made popular by England's Queen Victoria and her German husband, Prince

Albert. But the biggest surge of popularity of holiday decorations had come from the publication of Charles Dickens's *A Christmas Carol* in 1843, a singular literary event that would forever change how England, and soon its present and former dominions around the globe, would celebrate the birth of Christ.[4]

Prayers, and plenty of them, were part of daily life in the Houston home. And there would have been an abundance sent up on Christmas day in 1850. Before the holiday meal Margaret surely offered gratitude for a litany of blessings, especially the four waiting to be fed, and she would have requested safe passage for their absent father, still making his way to the northeast.

Sam Houston—waiting at an inn in Alexandria, Louisiana, that night for the next morning's stage, having made slow progress on his journey[5]—would likely have been grateful that the particularly tumultuous year, at times equally exhilarating and disappointing, and finally totally exhausting, was nearly done. He hadn't yet sorted out all that he needed to do regarding his standing with the Almighty or with religion in general. But he would have counted his wife and children as credits in his celestial ledger. And Texas, of course. And the Union. The luminaries on the national horizon were falling away—his old adversary Calhoun was already gone; Clay and Webster couldn't be far behind—and Houston might have requested a hint of divine insight regarding where he might end up in the altered grand scheme of things.

On one other matter, he had definite cause to render gratitude. In late November the Texas legislature, figuring putting paid to their old war debt was worth handing over a huge section of the state, even to a nation they were becoming increasingly unhappy with, had begrudgingly ratified the section of the federal compromise bill that depended on its endorsement.

But Houston must have realized that the nation, even with all of Senator Clay's proposals now firmly in place, had barely weathered the storm and that the great compromise was at best a patchwork affair. Perhaps it was enough of one, he must have hoped on that Christmas night, to hold the Union together for a time.

Two hundred miles away Margaret might have saved one of her most persistent invocations until the children were all asleep: that her husband would eventually consent to be baptized and place himself in the sure hands of a higher power than men could conjure or any of their governments could provide, a plea so common that it would have come as naturally to her as breathing. And she might have added a codicil that she would have doubtlessly considered selfish: that Houston come home for good and stay clear of politics and high society for the rest of his days, content to live happily with his family within their picket fence.

But surely Margaret realized, by then, that God sometimes grants one blessing while withholding another.

Part Two

1857–1863

The Union is worth more than Mr. Lincoln.

Thirteen

On May 12, 1857, a Tuesday, a traveling salesman named Ed Sharp rattled into Huntsville in a two-horse bright red buggy with a bold advertisement for his single inventory item, "Warwick's Patent Plow," painted on the side.[1] On learning that this was the home of the hero of San Jacinto, he asked the proprietor of the hotel as he was registering where the senator lived. The owner led him outside to the corner of the courthouse square and pointed down the long hill toward Woodland.

At the conclusion of a pleasant walk after a day's jostling in his buggy, he asked the man in his mid-sixties, outfitted in no telling what sort of colorful get-up, who met him at the gate if he had the honor of addressing General Houston.

"You have, young man," Houston told him, according to Sharp's reminiscences in a Dallas newspaper a quarter of a century later, "what can I do for you?"

"Nothing, General," the salesman replied. "If you are Sam Houston the object of my mission has been accomplished, as I only desired to see Sam Houston."[2]

Ever susceptible to flattery, Houston brought him inside and introduced him to Margaret, telling her he had just received a better compliment than any he had ever gotten on the Senate floor. Then they probably fed him. They seem to have fed anybody who showed up.

A little while later Houston, needing to reserve a place on the next stage heading down to the city seventy miles to the south that was named for him, accompanied Sharp as he walked back up the hill to the hotel, which also served as the stage office.[3] Houston told him that he had met with several friends the night before who had convinced him to toss his hat into the upcoming gubernatorial election. Just that morning he had written to his fellow Texas senator Thomas Rusk, informing him of his decision. Now he needed to get to a printer in Houston City to arrange for the publication of a schedule of his campaign speeches.[4]

The notion of the "friends" coming up with the idea of a run at the governorship is unlikely. He had surely mulled over the idea for a while, picking away at it like he whittled away at little pieces of wood before making up his mind. Assembling a few trusted acquaintances in the circle of straight-back chairs—one of them conspicuously empty; Henderson Yoakum had died the previous November—in his office at the corner of the yard would not have been to entertain a suggestion or probably even to seek their opinions regarding one he had already made. It would have been merely an opportunity to have his new scheme endorsed, the approval of a Greek chorus standing in the wings, not center stage.

Since everyone assumed that this would be his last Senate term, there had been considerable speculation that he would take aim at either the White House in Washington or the Governor's Mansion in Austin. For, much as his wife might want it so, everybody else seriously doubted that such an old political animal would be easily put out to pasture.

On May 4 the Texas Democratic convention in Waco had nominated Lieutenant Governor Hardin Runnels, the owner of a cotton plantation and an adamant proponent of states' rights, and inserted a carefully worded plank in their platform condemning Houston for his voting record in the Senate.[5]

The distance between what Houston saw as good for the Union and what the citizens and their elected officials in Texas deemed, in league with all the southern states, good for their region had grown continuously wider over the years. His support of the Oregon Bill in 1948, pro-Union appeals during the long debates over the Compromise Bill in 1850, and his constant defense of Indian rights had all set him in a place apart from that of the rest of the southern senators.

Then in 1854 he had made several impassioned Senate speeches in opposition to a piece of legislation proposed by Stephen Douglas, the Illinois Democrat who had herded the various pieces of Henry Clay's great compromise though the Senate in 1850 and was currently the chairman of the Committee on Territories. If passed, his bill would lump the land west of Missouri and Iowa into what would be known as the Kansas and Nebraska Territory. Douglas's stated purpose of the bill was to open up a wide swath to accommodate a transcontinental railroad. But the fact that the new entity would be allowed to make up its own mind regarding slavery, thus nullifying the Missouri Compromise of thirty years before, would give Douglas—a formidable, bellicose statesman known as the

"Little Giant" with the presidency in his sights—the much-needed support of southern members of his own party.[6]

Douglas might have seen the slavery issue as a moot point since cotton and other crops thriving in Dixie couldn't be successfully grown in that region. But what he would have also foreseen was that southern leaders could shove hordes of immigrants into the new territories, with IOUs promising future votes in their pockets, thus bettering the odds of several future slave states.

In his speeches Houston, totally opposed to any legislation that would repeal the Missouri Compromise, waged a two-pronged argument against passage, neither of which had anything to do with slavery, since he still defended the practice as essential to the economy of the South and falling only within the regulatory powers of each individual state.

First, he maintained that territories, not being elevated to the full status of statehood, could not decide such matters for themselves. And, second, much of that sprawling expanse of land had already been promised to Indians in perpetuity. Negating that pledge would make the federal government "Indian givers," a term meaning to take back a gift that was first coined in the eighteenth century and lived on in schoolyard arguments well into the twentieth.

"It is not novel for me to seek to advocate the rights of the Indians upon this floor and elsewhere," he began, stating the obvious since he had long been a champion of Native Americans. Then he gave his brethren a little history lesson. "Successive promises were made from 1785 to 1802," he lectured, "during the administration of General Washington, and the pledges of amity and regard that were made to the Indians by him, inured to Mr. Jefferson, for he, in 1809, made solemn promises to them, provided they would migrate west of the Mississippi." He then stated that it seemed to have become a "foregone conclusion that the Indians must yield to the progress of the white man," the great nations having been "driven like wild beasts" from place to place.[7]

Senators likely rolled their eyes or drummed their fingers on their desks during the diatribe, not because they felt any of its intended guilt but because they had heard it all from him before on numerous occasions. But they heard it again, when he stood and proclaimed the Indian in possession of "a sense of justice, truth, and honor that should find a responsive chord in every heart."[8]

Knowing full well that such sentiments wouldn't find that chord in many hearts present, southern or northern, he probably wasn't at all surprised that the Kansas-Nebraska Bill eventually passed easily. Even so, the South would never forgive him for his opposition to it, and it provided the proverbial straw that broke the camel's back for the Texas state legislature, which had reelected him to his third term in the Senate only the year before. There was absolutely no doubt in anyone's mind, including the senator's, that it would be his swan song.

So with three years left in Washington, he surveyed the political landscape. Having served as the commanding general of the army of the revolution, twice the president of the old republic, and as senator since 1846, the office of the chief executive was the last golden ring for him to grab in Texas.

In his letter to Thomas Rusk, written just that morning before the awestruck plow salesman showed up at his doorstep, he began by predicting his fellow senator's probable surprise at his announcement, knowing that he had intended to retire to private life. He went on to place the blame squarely on the Texas Democrats, who, with their "anti-Houston" foolishness, had shut him out of consideration for the nomination for governor of the state when five years before they had nominated him for president of the nation. "So now the whip cracks," he concluded, "& the longest pole will bring down the persimmon. The people want excitement, and I had as well give it as anyone."[9]

And he would give it as simply Sam Houston, not as a Democrat, a Know-Nothing (a fringe party he had briefly teased and flirted with), or anything else. He figured if voters didn't know what he stood for—and against—by now, a party platform wasn't likely to offer any clarity.

At the hotel, when Houston learned the next day's stage was fully booked, Ed Sharp mentioned that he was heading down to Houston City himself in the morning and wouldn't mind a little company. Having taken an instant liking to the young man, Houston accepted his offer.

Along the way they stopped in the town of Montgomery, where Houston made the first speech of his campaign. It wouldn't have been scheduled or advertised, since he had just made his final decision to run. But he could always come up with a few words, and usually many more than a few, wherever a crowd gathered. To the plow salesman's surprise—and delight—when the speech was concluded, part of the audience gathered around his scarlet buggy and began asking about the farming implement he was selling on order. Opportunist that he was, the young entrepreneur knew a win-win situation when he saw one.

When they resumed their journey south, Sharp let go of the reins, gave the horses their heads, and looked over the list of dozens of towns where Houston planned to speak throughout the summer. Figuring he would come into contact with more farmers in a single week in those gatherings than he could otherwise in an entire month, he offered himself as the senator's chauffeur.[10]

Houston, probably more intrigued by the prospect of somebody to talk to on the journey than by the money he would save on stage coaches or livery stables, made enough of a slight protest about Sharp being much too kind for the young fellow to assure him that he would be getting the better end of the bargain. So they struck a deal.

Back home in Huntsville, Houston spent the next two weeks mailing out his itinerary to newspapers—nearly every community had a daily or weekly publication; some had two, dependent on the political leanings of the publishers—and writing to prospective supporters in the towns where he would be speaking.

The excursion, winding though more than forty counties, would be arduous for a sixty-four-year-old whose several wounds from wars fought years before gave him trouble when he rode too long. But he was no stranger to lengthy, difficult journeys, having made his fair share of them between Huntsville and Washington over the last decade. Besides, it would be an adventure. And he was still up for an adventure, especially now that he had a youthful companion lined up whom he could regale with a vast repertoire of stories that his older acquaintances had already heard numerous times. The idea of a fresh campaign, a new battle to wage, probably provided sufficient adrenaline to make the old soldier downright giddy.

And the way the weather vane was tilting in the nation would have factored into his decision to run. The southern states, including his own, were committed to racing headlong toward secession, while many northern abolitionists were inclined to let such an exodus blow slavery, and those who supported it, out of the nation like a foul wind.

The Compromise of 1850 had finally proved too feeble a vessel to hold both factions. If—more likely *when*—war came, Houston believed that there should be a steadier hand than Runnels's on Texas' rudder to steer its course. And he had no doubt whatsoever whose hand that should be.

• • •

Just where Margaret stood on this sudden leap into state politics is unclear. Several of Houston's many biographers seem to concur that she readily agreed to it. Houston himself claimed, in the *Austin State Gazette* on July 25, 1857, that the ultimate decision had been hers. But Margaret's biographer, William Seale, concluded that she probably consented to her headstrong husband's foregone determination rather than have her differing opinion ignored.[11]

Either way, she would have worked her way through the positives and negatives. If elected, her long-absent husband would at least be back in Texas, not half a continent away. His term in the Senate wouldn't end until 1859, and he had no intention of resigning unless he was successful in this race. But, if successful, he wouldn't be returned to hearth and home exclusively, which had been Margaret's hope and prayer for all of their marriage. Their flock had grown to six children by now—Antoinette (Nettie) had arrived in January 1852, and Andrew Jackson Houston, two and half years later in June 1854—and she wanted her husband home, seeing to his household rather than a government.

She had scored decisive victories in two of the three battlefronts established when she was a young bride: to purge alcohol from his life, to deliver him into the Christian—specifically Baptist—religion, and to bring him out of the swirl of politics and public service to be a full-time husband and father.

Houston had sworn off liquor years before, apparently only relapsing the one time, in his skirmish with the Lockharts' bedpost. In fact, he had been an active and extremely popular speaker at temperance meetings in the Northeast, juxtaposing his old, often inebriated self to his new, upright one. Such gatherings were all the rage, from small church houses in tiny towns to huge auditoriums in the nation's largest cities, filled with fervent teetotalers as committed to their cause as hand-waving, amen-shouting flocks at tent revivals were to theirs.

Whether his participation in those rallies was entirely sincere is uncertain. He might truly have been the embodiment of the old adage about converts being the most passionate activists. But the politician in him had to have seen the golden opportunity to speak to large enthusiastic audiences made up of men who would be voting in the presidential election in a few years.[12]

Margaret's second conquest had occurred in November 1854, when he finally—after long discussions with family friend Reverend George Washington Baines (the great-grandfather of the yet-unborn future president Lyndon Baines Johnson) about Houston's misgivings regarding several sticky theological points—had consented to be baptized. A large crowd gathered to watch the immersion, after which someone congratulated him on his sins having been washed away. "I hope so," Houston responded, still drenched from his dunking, "but if they were *all* washed away, the Lord help the fish down below."[13]

That left only the third item on her list to be checked: to get him home for good. Beginning to wonder if there was any chance of it, she had even agreed, several years earlier, to consider a conciliatory "take the mountain to Muhammad" plan to move the entire family—probably minus Margaret's mother, though that decision would surely have been ceded to the indomitable Nancy Lea—to Washington. Houston had occasionally suggested such a move, but Margaret had never cottoned to the idea. She accepted the fact that Houston had no intention of resigning his Senate seat, though his promises to do so had come with the regularity of the changing seasons over the years.

She loved her Huntsville home and was leery of Washington society, and stepping onto so grand and busy a stage, while easy for Houston, would have proven extremely difficult for her. But after her trial and the flurry of gossip regarding Virginia Thorne and what she must have considered the betrayal of some of her friends over the matter, she seemed ready to put Huntsville behind her, at least for a while.

"I would like for you to select a pleasant boarding house about 8 or 10 miles from the city [Washington]," she wrote to Houston in early February 1851. "There are many arguments in favor of a country home, one which would weigh greatly with me, is that at night I would have your company, without being so much interrupted by visitors. Many others will suggest themselves to your mind."[14]

But the plan to relocate had never come to fruition, and Margaret and the children had stayed put in Texas. And now this intention to run for the state's highest office would mean, if he won, that the family would be expected to live in the Governor's Mansion, across the road from the State Capitol in Austin. And she had done more packing up and moving lately than she had wanted to.

In 1853 Houston rented out Woodland and moved the family to Independence, a town a few miles west of Washington-on-the-Brazos. One reason would have been so Sam Jr. could attend the preparatory academy that was part of Baylor College, a Baptist institution founded seven years before in Independence. Another was that Nancy Lea had bought a home and settled there, so Margaret could be in close proximity to her mother.

Two years later Houston packed up the family again and moved them to Cedar Point, the farm on Galveston Bay that had been Margaret's and his first home together, which she had optimistically named Ben Lomond. Shortly thereafter the family renting Woodland moved out, so the nomadic Houstons returned to Huntsville, which Margaret had probably never wanted to leave in the first place.

While the prospect of having the family together again on a permanent basis was appealing, another move and another high office were not. Austin was not Huntsville, the governor's residence was not Woodland, and Sam Houston running the entire state was a far cry from him bouncing his children on his knee and asking if there would be pie for supper.

Senator Sam Houston, 1850s. Courtesy Sam Houston Memorial Museum Collection.

Margaret Lea at the time of her wedding. Courtesy Sam Houston Memorial Museum Collection.

Houston near the end of his life. Courtesy Sam Houston Memorial Museum Collection.

Margaret Houston, 1860s. Courtesy Sam Houston Memorial Museum Collection.

Sam Houston Jr. Courtesy Sam Houston Memorial Museum Collection.

Nannie Houston, whom her mother predicted would be a "perfect romp." Courtesy Sam Houston Memorial Museum Collection.

Portrait of Nancy Lea by George Allen, ca. 1850. From the Collections of The Heritage Society, Houston, Texas.

Houston's law office in Huntsville on the grounds of the Woodland home. Courtesy Sam Houston Memorial Museum Collection.

The Houstons' Woodland home in Huntsville. Courtesy Sam Houston Memorial Museum Collection.

The Steamboat House, where Houston died in the first-floor room behind the stairs. The house was relocated from its original location in 1936, the centennial of Texas' independence from Mexico, to sit beside the Woodland home. Courtesy Sam Houston Memorial Museum Collection.

Sam Houston's original tombstone. Courtesy Sam Houston Memorial Museum Collection.

The 1911 monument by Pompeo Coppini at Sam Houston's grave. Courtesy Sam Houston Memorial Museum Collection.

Fourteen

Ed Sharp showed up in town again in late May, and he set off with Houston for Crockett, a town in fittingly named Houston County, just fifty miles north of Huntsville and the site of Houston's first stop on the much-publicized speaking schedule. And thus began one of the most interesting road trips in the history of Texas.

The morning after the Crockett speech they rode through dense piney woods into Cherokee County for two scheduled stops in that many days in Alto and in Rusk, a town named for Houston's Senate partner. The following day, May 30, Senator Rusk himself was much on Houston's mind, for the speech that day would be in Nacogdoches, Rusk's hometown and, during his first years in Texas, Houston's as well.

He had gotten word in Alto that Rusk intended to endorse Runnels, a bit of news that caused him to wonder, according to Ed Sharp's recollection, if his old friend had suddenly become his enemy.[1] The probable explanation was that Rusk, a loyal Democrat, would naturally endorse the candidate of his party. But Houston, who had long ago distanced himself from the Democrats and refused to be fettered by any ideology other than the holy trinity comprising Jacksonian democracy, the Union, and Texas would have seen Rusk's action as a betrayal.

He sent a note to Rusk, who was home from Washington for the congressional summer recess, asking if he could have a few moments of his time before he spoke. So the stage was set in Nacogdoches for a face-off of sorts.

It being a Saturday, the county seat was full of folks from outlying smaller communities and farms in town to tend to their weekly commerce and, this particular week, to hear what old Sam had to say and probably to see what outfit he showed up in. His attire would have been a disappointment, after the jutting sombreros and splashy Indian blankets he sometimes favored. For this trek through the broiling Texas summer he favored a white linen garment called a duster, a loose-fitting, lightweight jacket, not unlike a modern-day lab coat that fell to below his knees.[2] What he wore beneath it, if anything, other than his trousers and boots is anybody's guess. He had been known, in younger days, to stand before crowds bare-chested, perhaps reverting to his youthful sojourns among the Cherokees.

A stage had been constructed in the center of town, and a committee greeted Houston at Sharp's buggy and led him to it. He had been advised by several friends, fearing a demonstration against him and the crowd's reaction to Rusk's endorsement of his opponent, to give Nacogdoches a pass and move on to San Augustine, his next scheduled event. But here he was, on time, ready to speak, and stepping up to the platform. At the opposite side, Senator Rusk stepped up also.

The large audience watched as the two men walked slowly to the center of the stage. When they met, they embraced and both broke into tears. Then they went down together, got into Rusk's buggy, and rode to his home.[3] The crowd, deprived of both of the speeches they had come to hear, probably jawed for a while and then went about their usual Saturday business or headed home themselves. Hopefully some of them ordered Warwick Patent Plows from Ed Sharp, who wouldn't see Houston again until he collected him at Rusk's house the next morning. The two embraced again on the porch and bid each other farewell, at least one of them unaware that it would be the last time they would ever meet.

Two months later Senator Thomas Rusk committed suicide.

• • •

The stream of personal correspondence that had flowed so briskly between Houston and Margaret while he was in Washington, and en route to or from there, over the last decade dried up completely during his two-month junket through the state with Sharp. If any letters were exchanged at all none seem to have survived. Since almost all of the towns they visited were county seats, there would have been post offices aplenty from which Houston could have sent notes to Huntsville. Maybe the fact that he was significantly closer to home than he had been in Washington and that Margaret knew what he was up to were sufficient reasons to remain incommunicado. More probably he was enjoying himself too much to write.

This adventure must have reminded him of his escapes from civilization with the Indians in his youth or his soldiering days, sleeping on the ground on most nights—it seems he and Sharp sprang for hotel rooms only when there was a downpour—eating suppers of boiled or fried bacon, beans, and cornpone cooked over a campfire. And the daily promise of a large crowd assembled in every new town to hear him speak, equal mixes of supporters and adversaries—both of which would have fueled his inner fire—would have, even given the jolting springs of the buggy and the hectic schedule, made the whole enterprise an enjoyable one.

What Margaret did in his absence is no mystery, for he had been absent for much of their marriage. It being midsummer, the meals at Woodland would have been served on a table set up in the open dogtrot porch or out on the lawn. If too few rainstorms visited, water would have to have been carried in from the spring and poured on Eliza's vegetables and Margaret's flowers, which suffered under the merciless and determined summer sun.

As did Margaret. She was nearly forty now, no longer the girl who had just tiptoed out of her teens when she had married. Having borne six children, she must have counted it a blessing that she wasn't carrying another one during the wretched dog days of summer, when any discomfort was a chore and pregnancy would have seemed a downright curse. She had delivered her brood—Sam Jr., Nannie, Maggie, Mary Willie, Nettie, and Andrew—over a span of a dozen years, which meant individual variations of moods and needs to be dealt with.

Fourteen-year-old Sam Jr. was quickly growing into the handsome young man who would soon have to find his own way in the giant shadow of a famous father whose expectations regarding his behavior and his studies were high. The boy tried hard to meet them. When he was five, his mother wrote to Houston that, after a winter storm in Huntsville, he had been determined to run in the snow, which he had heard his father talk about doing during his early childhood in Virginia. She recounted that "he had taken up the idea that he could never be a man until he had done the same."[4]

The boy's natural creativity and sensitivity, much akin to his mother's, raised a warning flag for Houston, who had often instructed Margaret in his many letters home over the years to keep the boy at his lessons and away from foolish diversions like novels and poems. Artwork seems to have been permissible when Sam Jr. was very young, and Houston had praised some of the sketches enclosed in Margaret's letters. But later he encouraged her not only to impose a precise time limit but to infuse it with some sort of regimentation that might work its way into other activities. "I only suggest that you have it in your control," he wrote from Washington when Sam Jr. was nine, "and let him know that he is dependent on you for the indulgence, and let him have stated hours to draw. I think it a good thing, to teach him method, when young. Teach him to dispose of his clothes at night, so that he could get up in the dark, lay his hand on them, and dress."[5]

So if the lad could gain some useful skill—like dressing in the dark—from drawing, in strict moderation, it was acceptable. But poetry was forbidden, both the reading or writing of it. Any thoughts from Sam Houston Jr. would come seriously, in prose and in complete, straightforward sentences free of whimsy and needless embellishment. The newest addition to the family, Andrew, would at not-yet four have been the neediest of the lot, requiring the constant attention of his mother and Eliza when he was hungry, dirty, or just feeling slighted by his older siblings.

The quartet of sisters that fell between the two boys filled up their own bedroom across the upstairs open breezeway from the boys' room. Nannie, as much like her father as Sam Jr. was like their mother, was as headstrong, opinioned, and unpredictable at ten as Houston had been at that age. In a letter dated June 18, 1850, when Nannie would have been just shy of four, Margaret wrote to Houston about an incident that occurred on Sam Jr.'s seventh birthday: "He had two little boys to dine with him, sons of our minister Mr. Baines. One of them, a beautiful black-haired lad very nearly Sam's age was so charmed with Miss. Nannie's rosy cheeks, that he crept up slyly and stole a kiss from her. The young lady walked out in silent indignation, in a few minutes returned with a double handful of flour, and very soon Master Baines' pretty black coat presented a perfect spectacle."[6]

One of Margaret's early impressions of her oldest daughter, made when she had been barely two, would eventually prove entirely accurate. She wrote to Houston that Nannie was as mischievous as ever and that he should not expect "to find her improved in this respect, when you return, for I think she will always be a perfect romp."[7]

Next in the descending line were Maggie, Mary Willie, and Nettie—nine, seven, and five—who probably followed along in Nannie's spirited wake, causing Margaret and the slave tsarina they all called Aunt Eliza to keep a wary eye in case one or another of them slipped out one of the gates of the picket fence. If they did wander astray, one of the slaves on the place would have taken them back to the house or kept an eye on them until they decided to go back on their own.

Throughout their marriage the Houstons kept about a dozen slaves at a time.[8] If there was a chain of command, Eliza would be at the top, probably using a couple of young female slaves to do her bidding in her kitchen. Next would come Joshua, who had been born, raised, and trained as a blacksmith on the Lea plantation in Alabama. Lea died when Joshua was twelve and left him, along with Eliza, to his daughter Margaret in his will.[9] When Joshua arrived in Texas with the newlywed Houstons, he quickly became a trusted and resourceful aide to his new master and was either given or assumed dominion of a sort over the field hands, gardeners, and shop workers of Woodland and at Raven Hill, where the Houstons still owned some land. From time to time he took several slaves down to Cedar Point to cut timber.

The overseer, who lived in a small cabin on the property, would have had the official authority to assign tasks to each slave. But Eliza and Joshua were most likely more involved in their day-to-day, moment-to-moment activities, a practice not unlike the head butler and the housekeeper occupying a unique middle ground between the upstairs family and downstairs servants in British manor houses of the same era. The glaring difference, of course, was that the English servants were free to move on when they found better pay, while slaves in America were held in bondage, weren't paid anything, and could be punished and sold according to their owners' whims.

Every slave knew the cruel reality of their lives and the seemingly hopeless prospects of future freedom, even the ones treated well like those in the Houston household. In March, only a couple of months before Houston began his cross-county junket, the Supreme Court, in *Dred Scott v. Sanford*, decreed that no black person, slave or free, could be an American citizen and defined slaves as property.

This meant, in the current political theatrics being played out, that their owners could move them into the western territories. It also meant, to the slaves, that they were now officially seen by the nation in which they lived as no more important than an acre of land, an implement to work it, the livestock that grazed on it, or a chair or a table in a room. Chief Justice Roger B. Taney hoped that the ruling would put an end to the slavery question that had been festering for years. Those slaves who knew about the decision would have seen it as the death knell of any hope of freedom.

• • •

One of the Houston's youngest slaves, Jeff, just three years older than Sam Jr., was as often a playmate of the children as he was doing chores assigned to him by Eliza. He came into the family by pure happenstance, when at age thirteen he crossed paths with Sam Houston. It proved to be a fortuitous meeting. Jeff was born in 1840 on the Kentucky plantation of Singleton Gibson who, three years later, sold out and moved his family to Texas, of course loading up and bringing his slaves—including Jeff, his mother, and her other children—with him along with his other possessions. The Gibsons settled just southwest of Houston City in Fort Bend County, where Gibson was killed soon after in some sort of skirmish with Indians. His widow promptly married a disagreeable fellow named McKell who favored violence and whiskey, each passion feeding the other and the recipients of the subsequent fury always his slaves.

The new head of the household moved it constantly from place to place, probably staying one step ahead of creditors, until landing in the backwoods of Trinity County, where he built a rough cabin with a lean-to. Jeff and his brothers and sisters shared a miserable hut with their mother, a large woman known to everyone, even her children, as Aunt Big Kittie.

Eighty-six years later, when he was almost one hundred, Jeff would remember that he and his family were "worked long hours, whipped, cursed, and half starved" by McKell.[10] The boy's eventual deliverance had been bittersweet and frightening. When McKell needed cash to pay off a debt for two barrels of whiskey that he had already consumed, he pounded on Aunt Big Kittie's door one predawn October morning and demanded she get Jeff up and dressed. A few minutes later the boy looked back from the departing wagon at his mother filling up the slave cabin's open doorway.

By late morning the little party—McKell, two of his adult slaves, and Jeff—rolled into Huntsville and came to a stop at Gibbs's Mercantile on the courthouse square. McKell told one of his slaves to offload the slave block—apparently some people traveled with their own, ready to conduct a quick sale and avoid paying the official auctioneer on the courthouse lawn a cut of the profit—and set it on the plank walkway in front of the store. In a minute Jeff was standing on the block and a crowd was gathering. McKell stepped forward and announced that he was offering "a little nigger for sale, cheap."[11]

Jeff, who hadn't been given any breakfast before being loaded up and carted off that morning, fixed his attention on fresh loaves of gingerbread in the store window. A gaggle of white boys teased and taunted him, a couple of them stepping up a few times as if to strike him. It was a warm, cloudless morning, and when the sun leveled off in the midday sky, it grew hot enough for McKell to take off his coat and vest. He pointed at Jeff and told the crowd that he was only eight and would one day make a "husky field hand."

If Jeff hadn't been so hungry, so tired of standing in the heat, and frightened to the point of fighting back tears, he might have smiled at that. He would later explain that McKell lied about his age because he figured he would never sell a "runty, small-fry boy like myself if bidders knew I was thirteen years old instead of eight. There were already too many house boys and gardeners, and if a buyer knew my real age, he would know that I would never grow into a big, strong slave."[12]

After a couple of hours, a bid of five hundred dollars was made by a man named Moreland. McKell couldn't get anyone to raise it, so he shook the man's hand, telling him he would have to have the cash soon enough for him to get back home to Trinity County before nightfall. Moreland told him he had to go home to get it, several miles south of town, and would be back soon.

No sooner had the dust settled from his departure than a buckboard buggy pulled by a huge black horse, the first buggy Jeff had ever seen, rolled to a stop at Gibbs's store. After he tied off the reins to the hitching post, the tall man who climbed down asked what all the commotion was about. "Nothing at all, General," somebody said, adding that it was just a slave boy being sold. Houston, a maker of laws and ever conscientious about seeing them enforced, walked over to McKell, called him "my friend," then asked if he didn't know that it was illegal to block the plank walk, adding that if he wanted to "put on a show," he ought to take his block over to the courthouse where it belonged.[13]

Before McKell could respond, Houston told him the boy was frightened and the group of white boys was scaring him. Then he asked if he had had a bid. When he heard about the five hundred dollars offered by Moreland, whom he knew to be a cruel slave master, he pointed at Jeff, still standing on the block, and asked how he could sell him to a "yellow dog" like that, apparently unaware that he was addressing a creature of the same stripe.

Not waiting for an answer he asked if the boy had any family back on McKell's place. When he heard about the mother and her other children, Houston became indignant. He said he would pay cash for the boy, provided McKell cut the price by fifty dollars and agree to sell him the rest of the family at a later date. Then, probably not waiting for a reply, he lifted Jeff down from the block and guided him into the first store the boy ever stood in. Houston asked Thomas Gibbs to give McKell the cash and charge it to his account and to give Jeff something to eat, then went off on some errand.[14]

When he returned, he picked out a wide-brimmed straw hat from Gibbs's selection and put it on Jeff's head. He told him he didn't need to be afraid anymore, that nobody was going to hurt him, and that he should wait there with Thomas Gibbs until a slave named Joshua came to collect him. Then he told him he had a little boy almost as old as him that he could play with, and he was gone as quickly as he had arrived.[15]

By the summer of 1857, when Houston was on his rambling campaign tour, Jeff was practically a member of the family, having provoked his new master's famous wrath only one time. When Nannie was a small child, Jeff had been told to look after her when they went down to the pond at Woodland so that Old Pete, one of Houston's horses, could get a drink. Nannie was carrying a switch she had pulled from a bush, and Jeff told her to swat the horse with it, knowing that it was a cantankerous animal and wanting to see his reaction. Old Pete reared up, and the little girl fell backward into the water.

When Houston heard the resulting caterwauling from his oldest daughter, he arrived just as Jeff was pulling her up on the shore. He gave the boy a whipping then and there.[16] It was apparently the only time that Sam Houston, who had strong-armed more than a few men and thrashed one in a Washington street with a cane, ever struck one of his slaves. The purchase of the rest of Jeff's family by Houston never transpired, McKell having apparently sold them off quickly to various families to raise ready cash. It would be a quarter of a century before Jeff would see his mother again.

Fifteen

From Nacogdoches Houston and Ed Sharp moved due east to San Augustine, then up to Shelbyville, a little burg on the Texas-Louisiana border. From there they headed north toward Carthage on June 4, riding slowly between looming walls of pine trees that bordered the rough road, the horses moving at not much more than a stroll. Houston, holding the reins, had been recounting his life story for Sharp and reached the point where he had married Eliza Allen in 1827. He stopped abruptly, and the two sat in silence for a time.

By then Houston and Sharp had sat beside several campfires, eaten camp suppers together, and sipped boiled coffee from tin cups under wide starry skies as Houston spun a few anecdotes and usually ended their long days with a song.[1] Then they spread out their blankets on the ground and slept before working the next day's crowd—one selling plows, the other selling himself.

A camaraderie had been established in just a few days that Sharp would have reason to fear, on the road to Carthage that morning, that he might have overestimated. He started to ask a question, and Houston pulled on the reins to stop the horses. "Go on, my young friend," he said.

"I fully realized," Sharp later recounted, "that he had anticipated what I was about to do. I frankly acknowledged to him that I was about to ask him a very delicate question concerning himself, but was not prompted by idle curiosity, but in consequence of the intense interest he himself had aroused in me."[2]

Then Houston asked if he admitted that he was about to ask why he had separated from his first wife. "I do, General, but I hope you will forgive me."

The response probably surprised him, for Houston said he not only forgave him but would "gratify" him. According to Sharp, Houston broke his long silence and related the story, significantly shorter than the several others he had heard from him. Referring to Eliza at eighteen as "one of the most beautiful, elegant, and accomplished ladies in Tennessee," he said that he had fallen in love with her and had believed the affection was "reciprocated." Not long after the fancy wedding he discovered that his young bride was awfully unhappy and learned either from her or others that she had been pushed by her social-climbing family into an attractive union with the governor of Tennessee rather than allow her to marry the young man she was in love with.

There is no record of Houston ever having mentioned the exchange, so we have only the word of Sharp, recalled a half century later and long after Houston's death. But whether or not it was relayed on that lonely road, the ill-fated sweethearts scenario seems the most viable regarding the series of events that sent Houston into his drunken anguish, back to the Indians and, eventually, into Texas.

James Haley, author of the Houston biography that is arguably the current standard reference, maintains that the importance of this revelation, if it occurred, had less to do with the old secret being shared with a plow salesman as with the fact that the issue had finally been put to rest. "The story had not changed," Haley says, "but Houston had changed; having the security now not just of Margaret but also of the church, he was finally at peace with the subject."[3]

• • •

From Carthage they headed west to Henderson and Tyler, then rolled through a wide backward arc to Gilmer and Marshall, up to Jefferson, and over a long westward swath across the top of the state through Dangerfield, Tarrant, Greenville, McKinney, and Alton. Then they dropped down to Birdville, the county seat of Tarrant County, which would eventually be absorbed by Haltom City, now a suburb of Fort Worth. Next came Dallas, roughly thirty miles to the east.

Crowds gathered at every stop, running the gamut from friendly to hostile, with some merely curious to see the great man himself, more interested in his nearly mythical past than his present politics. Each speech lasted usually from two to three hours and was pretty much the same as any other.[4] He gave no speeches on Sundays, hoping to avoid the displeasure of both God and Margaret.

One or another of his plentiful political enemies would usually take to the stump after he was done, a carefully orchestrated tactic of the Democrats to produce a slate of speakers to urge audiences to elect Runnels and roll off a catalogue of reasons not to vote for Houston. He refused to share the platform with any of them and always took his leave before they began. Though a skilled debater, he chose that summer to distance himself completely from the political party that had both abandoned and banished him, presenting his qualifications and agenda directly to the people and not wasting his time arguing with distracters. But, being the scrapper he was, he found opportunities to get his licks in.

In Tyler one of his oldest and most determined foes, State Representative and fire-eating secessionist Louis Wigfall, was scheduled to speak after him. As he was closing, Houston told the crowd that a "murderer named Wiggletail"—Wigfall had killed a man in a duel years before—was about to talk and that he advised them not to listen unless they were "fond of lies."[5]

From Dallas Sharp and Houston followed a decidedly southeastern route through Waxahachie, Corsicana, Fairfield, Centerville, and Madisonville, giving speeches and taking orders for plows along the way, and finally rolled into Huntsville at midnight on July 3. After a big Independence Day celebration and barbecue the next day, with Huntsville's most famous resident—though hardly the town's favorite son at the moment—as the main speaker, the campaign took a brief hiatus to provide a bit of time with Margaret and the children.

They lit out again on the eighth, a Wednesday, stopping first in the little town of Anderson, a short distance west of Huntsville. Then the scarlet buggy rattled northwest through Boonville, Wheelock, and Marlin to Waco, where the Democrats had nominated Runnels and publicly castigated Houston a few months before, and finally due south through Cameron, Caldwell, La Grange, and then up to Austin, where he spoke in a grove of trees close to the Capitol. That there was no love lost between Houston and the city of Austin was common knowledge. Some of the bad blood went back to his comments in 1840 about the absurdity of placing the seat of government in a remote little village far removed from where most Texans lived and susceptible to attacks by Plains Indians.

But what stuck most in Austin's citizens' craws was what had come to be called the Archives War. In 1842 Houston, in his second term as president of the republic, had decided the government should relocate to Houston City when Mexican forces invaded nearby San Antonio. He ordered all official files and documents to be loaded into wagons and moved to the temporary capital for safekeeping. Some Austin folks, fearing that he intended to use the opportunity to make his namesake city the permanent capital, formed a vigilante brigade intent on keeping the records where they figured they belonged.

Houston sent in a company of Texas Rangers with orders to escort the numerous wagons and with strict orders not to resort to bloodshed. One resolute partisan, Angelina Eberly, managed to fire a cannon in the general direction of the departing convoy. The parade had not made it twenty miles before the committee, with either the cannon Eberly had somehow come by or another one, overtook the many wagons at Kenny's Fort on Brushy Creek. A few shots were fired by the mob, but it's uncertain if the cannon was discharged. The Rangers, following President Houston's orders, did not return fire and watched the vigilantes hijack the wagons and return the archives to Austin, where they stayed until the government moved back into town for good.[6]

Given the tempestuous relationship between the city and the man whose goal was to move into its Governor's Mansion, it's no wonder the reviews of his speech by the city's broadsheets were scathing. The *Star Gazette* reported that there were "many empty benches" by the time Houston finished talking and concluded that the entire address had been "a melancholy picture of imbecility, vindictiveness and hate in old age." Houston's response was that John Marshall, the paper's editor, would not eat meat—apparently vegetarianism was a cardinal sin in Houston's estimation—and "one drop of his blood would freeze a frog."[7]

The next day, having shaken the dust of Austin and its bad press off his feet and traveled to nearby Lockhart, Houston learned that his adversary this time would be Williamson Oldham, an old foe. They had known each other in Arkansas when Oldham was a state legislator and Houston was living in the Indian Territory. Neither had been at their best in those days—Oldham had fallen from respectability because of alleged financial shenanigans involving destroying incriminating bank records, and Houston had fallen deep into drink. They had not liked each other.

They still didn't.

Oldham arrived at the rally shortly before Houston concluded his talk and began unpacking big bound volumes of Senate records containing Houston's speeches from which he intended to read verbatim Houston's support of the Union to the crowd. When Houston noticed the audience beginning to whisper and point, he saw a grand opportunity for some showmanship. Always up for a bit of high drama—the stage would have gained a fine actor had he not gone in for soldiering and politics—he told the crowd to be still, that he would see what the commotion was about. He took his time walking to the side of the platform and gazing at his old acquaintance lifting out the hefty tomes.

Back at stage center he gave his report. "It's Oldham, only Oldham. I'll tell you what he's doing." He stepped back to his vantage point and looked again, probably lifting one hand dramatically over his eyes, like Ahab gazing out over the briny deep for a glimpse of Moby Dick. Then he stepped back to the front. "He is opening some books," he explained. "But they are not the bank books he stole and sunk in White River, Arkansas." At which point Oldham, according to one witness's recollection, bit the cigar he was smoking in half.[8]

• • •

From Austin the traveling duo, well seasoned by then but surely exhausted, headed west to San Marcos; south again to Seguin (named for the alcalde—mayor—of San Antonio at the time of the siege of the Alamo); across to New Braunfels, full of enough German immigrants for them to find sausages, sauerkraut, and perhaps a beer or a shot of schnapps for Sharp; and then into San Antonio on Tuesday, July 28.

By the thirtieth they were in Gonzales, and the first day of August found them in Victoria, the southernmost point of their long pilgrimage and the final scheduled stop on their itinerary. From there they made a northeastern trek to Huntsville, apparently making no stops to give speeches and sell plows. By the time the red buggy rolled into town at the end of the first week of August, the election had already taken place.

Their trek—covering more than two months, forty-three events in forty-one counties, and an estimated fifteen hundred miles—when plotted out on a map of the eastern half of Texas resembles a top-heavy giant figure eight, with Huntsville at the bisecting hub.

It took much of the rest of the month for all the results to make their way to Austin from the far-flung reaches of the sprawling state. When all the ballots were tallied and confirmed, Runnels had garnered 32,552 votes to Houston's 28,678, which didn't constitute a thrashing but did hand Houston the only defeat of his political career.[9]

Though it had to have stung, he attempted to put the best possible face on it. In a letter to Ashbel Smith in Galveston he said that if it were not such a disappointment for his friends, he would rejoice at the result since he would now return to the Senate. It's highly doubtful, after the long two months of hard campaigning and the evident disapproval registered by his fellow Texans, that he truly rejoiced. But he did pull himself up from any sulking he might have done and determined to look forward, not back.

"The fuss is over," he told Smith in his letter, "and the sun yet shines as ever." He concluded by saying that he still had "other fish to fry."[10] To his wife, he gave a more specific indication of one of the fish he had in mind. "Margaret," he told her, probably dashing any hope she still clung to of him stepping finally out of his world into hers, "wait until 1859,"[11] which was the year of the next gubernatorial election in Texas.

Sixteen

One of the first items on Houston's agenda when he returned to Washington in early 1858 was to pay homage to his recently deceased fellow Texas senator Thomas Jefferson Rusk. They had often disagreed in the dozen years since the state legislature had sent them to the capital, but they had shared a mutual civil respect, hovering perhaps between friendship and tolerance, that went back to the war for independence from Mexico in 1836.

In that tempestuous and pivotal year they were both signers of the Texas Declaration of Independence. Less than a month later Interim President David Burnet, angered at Houston's galloping retreat from Santa Anna's army after the fall of the Alamo, sent Rusk, his secretary of war, to order Houston to halt what history would later record as the Runaway Scrape and make a stand. When Houston told Rusk, his superior, that he suspected Santa Anna intended to capture the government at Harrisburg, Rusk decided to allow the general to continue his retreat until he could catch the Mexican force unaware. Then they both fought valiantly at San Jacinto. When Houston was elected the new republic's first president, he chose Rusk as his own secretary of war.[1]

Despite their differences in the Senate, their emotional last meeting at Nacogdoches during Houston's campaign swing through Texas had apparently settled things amicably, maybe because Rusk knew it was the final opportunity to do so. The cause of his suicide was never known, though it was commonly assumed that his wife's recent death of tuberculosis and his own illness—he had a painful tumor on the base of his neck—were contributing factors.

Houston's enemies gladly added the increased workload on Rusk because of Houston's attention to his gubernatorial campaign and possible presidential run as part of the reason. As early as the previous September, less than two months after the suicide, Houston's secretary John Williams wrote to him from Washington that "the hounds want to make out that you murdered Rusk," adding that an article in the *Philadelphia Press* was "damnable."[2]

Houston's tribute on the Senate floor was eloquent and no doubt sincere. "As a soldier he was gallant," he said, "his chivalry spotless, his honor clear; as a statesman he was wise, conservative, and patriotic; as a friend, he had all the high qualities that ennoble the heart; . . . as a man, he had all the qualities that adorn human nature." In closing, Houston predicted that Rusk would be remembered in the Senate and beyond: "He will be remembered throughout the nation; he will be unforgotten in Texas whilst either history or tradition lives."[3]

Rusk's death closed yet another chapter in Houston's life. Even while enjoying the good fortune of having a devoted wife and a houseful of healthy children, with another on the way, he must have felt the loneliness for absent friends that comes naturally with a long life. He was nearly sixty-five, having exceeded the average life expectancy in America in his era by a decade and more. And the list of friends and loved ones he had outlasted grew ever longer.

He sat vigil at his mother's deathbed in 1831; three years later Oolooteka, the Cherokee chief who had been such a strong influence in his boyhood, died. The war that resulted in Texas' independence claimed Austin, Travis, Crockett, Bowie, Fannin, Milam, and many others. He arrived at the Hermitage just a few hours after his mentor, Andrew Jackson, died in 1845 and was a member of the Senate honor guard that escorted Henry Clay's body home to Kentucky in 1852. Two years later his favorite sister Polly died, as did his close friend Henderson Yoakum in 1856.

With all those doors closing, along with the nagging discomfort of his old injuries from the War of 1812 and San Jacinto that had never properly healed, he must have often sensed what the poet Andrew Marvell called "time's winged chariot drawing near."[4] Although he couldn't avoid its inevitability, he seemed determined to outrun his assailant as long as possible.

Not content to be a lame duck in the final year of his last term, he seemed set on becoming even more of a force to be reckoned with, and he had never been shy about making his voice heard. In short, he would not go quietly. When he lost the governor's race, many Texans expected him to do what they considered to be the honorable thing and resign from the Senate. His replacement, former chief justice of the Texas Supreme Court John Hemphill, had already been elected; though his term wouldn't begin for another year, he waited patiently in the wings for Houston to step aside.[5] He would have a long wait. Stepping aside had never been one of Houston's strong suits.

Instead, he became a whirling dervish of energy. He rose to make points of order whenever an opportunity presented itself. He rose to move that the Senate abolish night sessions. He rose to suggest sending young male volunteers into Utah to lure potential wives away from the Mormons, seeing it as the best way to "break up the whole establishment; it will take away their capital." He constantly rose to request time to refute or clarify or object or question.[6] When he wasn't on his feet, he whittled and wrote letters, most of them to Margaret and the children. The piles of pine shavings rose at his feet; pages had to bring more sheets of foolscap on which he could scratch his missives.

In one to his oldest daughter, Nannie, who was nearly twelve, he waxed philosophical about how children shouldn't feel slighted or envious if one of their siblings received a gift that the others didn't or one of more value. Sam Jr. would be happy with a model rifle, he explained, while Andrew would be much more content with a "dog knife." And Nannie's younger sisters would be delighted with something as simple as "candy, or sugar plums." What Nannie had or hadn't received that prompted this dispatch wasn't mentioned, but her father finally worked his way around, through the usual field of unnecessary commas, to some advice: "Children ought to be careful, not to draw any opinion, from such facts, until they reflect well on them. And above all things," he advised, sounding awfully like Polonius in his speech to his children in *Hamlet*, "discard envy nor ever indulge bad temper. If there is any thing on earth, that is of all thing[s] most unamiable in woman, it is bad temper." At the end he told her he was enclosing some apple seeds to plant or "divide with the neighbors."[7]

Perhaps it was an allegorical gesture meant to encourage Nannie to plant the seed of his shared wisdom and nurture it to fruition. Or he might have felt the need to send her a little something in recompense for whatever gift she had not gotten, or appreciated, in the first place. One must wonder if he had the convenient seeds in his Senate desk or his pocket, or if he sent one of the pages out to fetch them.

When he wasn't writing letters or whittling, he was again upright, seeking recognition from whoever was sitting in the big armchair under the scarlet canopy. He railed against increasing the size of the army in a time of peace. What his home state needed, he said, was not more federal soldiers but more Texas Rangers, funding for a thousand of them to be exact, to protect the southern border. "Texas does not want regular troops," he told the Senate, waving them away with his big hand. "Withdraw them if you please."[8]

That border, fully one-half of the dividing line between the United States and Mexico, must have been much on his mind, as evidenced in his next ploy, which took everyone completely by surprise. In February he put down his whittling, rose to his feet at his desk, and introduced a resolution proposing the establishment of a US protectorate over "the so-called Republic of Mexico."[9] While his colleagues sat silently and probably wide eyed, he began what would be a total of six speeches advocating the bold move, facing overwhelming disinterest each time. The crux of his argument was that Mexico's government was a complete mess after twenty-five revolutions in twenty-eight years and that the ongoing chaos would eventually lead to the country being "turned over to barbarism."[10] What Mexico needed, he seemed to be advocating, was a calm, wise pilot to take over the steerage of its course. Both nations would benefit, he asserted, and peace would finally abide between the two.

The United States stepping up as a compassionate friend of its southern neighbor wasn't the only thing on his mind, of course. Other than his tunnel-visioned and adamant dedication to keeping the Union intact, there had rarely been a case when he had kept just one scheme brewing. The most obvious example was that even as he had fought vigorously to wrench Texas away from Mexico in 1836 and make it an independent republic, he had at the same time been charting the best and speediest path to deliver Texas into the Union as a state.

He had to have realized that the Senate wasn't about to endorse sending an army down to Mexico to announce that it was now in charge, any more than the Mexican government, whichever one was currently seated, would welcome the idea. A complete military takeover would have to be waged, and the United States hadn't yet taken up empire building.

But he at least established the fact that conquering or uniting—absorbing would be more in line with his thinking—with Mexico was on his mind, already factoring the future possibility into whatever he envisioned after his final Senate term was completed and he returned home to Texas.

For there is no doubt what he saw as the future. "I think it very probable," he said in one of his several speeches on his proposal, "that our extreme southern border will soon extend to the city of Mexico."[11] It's unclear if he was speaking of the Texas border or the nation's. But it is crystal clear which one the sitting president, James Buchanan, had in mind. He had told Congress in 1858 that it was "beyond question, the destiny of our race to spread themselves over the continent of North America."[12]

Whatever President Buchanan might have thought of the protectorate scheme, it went nowhere fast. So Houston fumed and whittled and finally moved on to those other fish he had promised to fry. In the spring he stepped headlong into the debates on the location of the much-anticipated transcontinental railroad that would finally provide an uninterrupted conduit between the far-flung eastern and western boundaries of the nation.

Three routes were being considered. The northernmost, through what is now Montana and Oregon, would pretty much follow the trail blazed by Lewis and Clark some sixty years earlier. The central, along what was part of the Oregon Trail, would pierce through Nebraska and southern Wyoming.[13] Houston, to no one's surprise, advocated the third plan, the southern route. The obvious advantage was that it, unlike the other two, completely avoided the Rocky Mountains and the colossal logistical difficulties they presented. But Houston favored it because it would go through Texas.

In the end, he got precious little he had fought for, finally able to claim only a single slight victory concerning his opposition to strengthening the military. "Some say I defeated it [the bill to increase the regular army]," he wrote to Margaret in February, adding that it was "lost in the Senate."[14]

His protectorate pitch was dead on arrival; in fact, it had quickly become the target of reproach and humor. One senator called it "a gross insult to Mexico," and another threatened, with tongue firmly embedded in cheek, to amend Houston's proposal "to extend the same inquiries to the Canadas and the other British possessions in our continent."[15]

The first transcontinental railroad would eventually follow the central route, as far north of the sweltering summer heat of Texas as it was south of the deep winter snows of Montana. Federal pay for more Texas Rangers was not forthcoming, no wife-seeking volunteers were dispatched to Utah to pilfer women from the Mormons, and the Senate apparently kept to the practice of having night sessions as often as it chose to have them.

In November the Texas legislature sent James Pinckney Henderson, who had served as the first governor of Texas, to replace Thomas Rusk in the Senate. There's not much evidence that he made much of a splash once he arrived, but whatever he accomplished was likely more than his fellow senator did.

Though he had almost another full year to serve Sam Houston had proved, in spite of valiant efforts on his part to the contrary, to be the lamest of ducks indeed. It must have seemed, to the Senate and to himself, like he had already left.

• • •

In Huntsville Margaret was ailing and had been for some time. The exact nature of her malady is unclear; she was pregnant again, but she had been that often enough. Though she alluded to her illness only briefly in the few letters she sent to Washington—barely a trickle of correspondence from her when compared to the continuous flood of the past dozen years—her two oldest children mentioned it in notes to their father.

"My dear Pa," Sam Jr. wrote in early December, "Ma received your letter from Alexandria [Houston posted it from Louisiana while on his way back to Washington] but was too unwell to answer it but she hopes to be well enough to write next mail." He then reported that he was making progress in his studies. Margaret added three short sentences at the bottom of the sheet, offering her apology for not being able to write that day.[16]

Several months later Nannie began her letter to "my dear Papa" with "Ma would have written but she felt too unwell." She told him that the catalpa tree he had planted himself was "covered with pretty large leaves and tolerable large bulbs." Having already told him how much she missed him, she closed with "Pa if your business did not require your presence longer in Washington I should be glad for you to hasten home with all possible speed. We are all anxious to see you. So make haste won't you?"[17]

As if complying with her summons, he arrived in the late spring for the last of his regular-as-clockwork biannual visits wedged between congressional sessions. He greeted the newest addition to his flock—third son, William Rogers Houston, had arrived in late May—and doled out hugs, kisses, and little gifts to the rest of the family, probably substituting a handshake for the more affectionate business to Sam Jr., who was, after all, fifteen.

At some point during his stay, amid the trips up to town and inspecting the grounds and spending as much time with his wife and children as he could, he announced his decision that the family would soon be leaving Huntsville for good and moving to their farm in Independence.

Where they would raise sheep.

Seventeen

The news about leaving Huntsville couldn't have come as a complete surprise. Houston and Margaret had actually sold Woodland the year before. The new owner, a friend of the family named J. Carrol Smith, had apparently been in no hurry to take possession of the property, and the Houstons stayed on knowing that at some future time they would have to leave.[1]

But the sheep plan was likely a shocker. Margaret must have seen the prospect as unlikely. She had been led down the gentleman-farmer-in-retirement road before, only to be abandoned with two small children out in the wilderness on Raven Hill in 1846.

The reason Houston gave for selling out in Huntsville was to settle the debt incurred during his speaking tour in the governor's race in 1857. At first glance there wouldn't seem much to need paying for. Ed Sharp had provided the transportation, and the two traveling companions had spent most nights during that two-month rambling odyssey sleeping on the ground after suppers cooked in a skillet over campfires.

But the bacon and beans in the skillet would have been provided by Houston. As would all the meat and fixings for the big barbecues held at most stops to draw crowds, the printing expenses for all the fliers, and the cost of running notices in every newspaper in every town.[2] And he had run as an independent, with no political party or machine to underwrite some or all of his expenditures. He was still drawing his Senate salary, but that would come to a grinding halt soon. So he was probably looking ahead, for once, to leaner days.

Much as he and Margaret loved the Huntsville homestead, it would have fetched the best price of his trio of properties. Whatever they had kept at Raven Hill had been sold by then, and that left only their farms at Independence and Cedar Point. Smith had paid four thousand dollars for Woodland—the house, outbuildings, and adjoining acreage—leaving the Houstons with no connection to Huntsville whatsoever.

Another reason for leaving might have had something to do with a disagreement Houston, as a member of the administrative board of Austin College, had with Reverend Samuel McKinney, the president of the school. McKinney resigned, apparently because of the conflict, and Houston may have been reluctant to enroll Sam Jr. there so soon after the bad business.[3]

Whatever the reason, it's difficult to think that Margaret was completely content with the transaction. There's no record of her objecting to the sale or voicing an opinion about it one way or the other. But most of her children had been born in her pretty house with its open hallway in the center. Every flower bed and fruit tree had been dug and planted by her or Eliza; every room and path and outlying meadow held specific memories. The white picket fence had enclosed her whole little life and world, to which she had always hopefully assumed her husband would one day return for good.

Now she would have to pack up everything for another move, something she surely hoped never to have to do again. And this time *everything* would have to go, unlike the other times when the family had simply set up short-term housekeeping in one of their other homes before returning to Huntsville. Even the rental of Woodland to another family in 1853 had been a temporary situation, and many of their possessions might have been left there.

Margaret had been ill for a while and hadn't completely regained her strength, already greatly diminished after recently giving birth. So the preparation and execution of such a grand exodus must have seemed particularly overwhelming. And there was the new baby to consider. Willie was a slight, sickly child—Margaret had called him a "pale little cripple" in a letter to Houston a couple of months after his birth[4]—and he would require more care and attention than his six older, healthier siblings had as infants. Even if there was no other reason to stay put, and there were plenty, Margaret would surely have rather tended to the family's newest arrival where she had become accustomed to tending to babies.

But, come what may, Houston had made his decision. The family spent some of the summer at Cedar Point, where Willie received regular baths in the warm, slowly lapping surf of Galveston Bay. The abundance of fresh sea air and bright sunshine, coupled with those healing immersions, were undoubtedly good for the infant and welcomed by his older brothers and sisters, out of school for the summer.

And their parents had each other, for one sun-splashed season before Houston returned to Washington for his final term in the Senate. And then? Margaret had probably long since stopped asking that question.

• • •

At some point during Houston's absence in Washington the yellow buggy Margaret had long claimed as her personal chariot sat hitched and ready in front of Woodland. Behind it stretched an impressive line of several wagons containing all manner of furniture, parcels, baskets, crock jars, crates, trunks, and barrels filled with the family's worldly goods. Mollie, Nettie, and Andrew—aged eight, six, and four—sat beside drivers or somewhere amid the neatly stowed cargo. Sam Jr., Nannie, and Maggie—aged fifteen, twelve, and ten—were already living with Margaret's mother in Independence and attending school there. The contingent of slaves made up the rest of the entourage. Eliza would have been in charge of those overseeing household goods and kitchen stores; Joshua, over those tending any livestock that hadn't been sold off and would be making the trip.

Margaret probably closed the little gate of the picket fence herself and latched it before taking her seat in the buggy, which would have been driven by young Jeff, her usual chauffeur. Either she or Eliza would have held Willie, wrapped snugly against the autumn weather. In a moment the convoy pulled slowly away from the handsome white house and its pretty grounds and headed up the hill to town, where in a few minutes it would turn left at the corner of the courthouse square at Gibbs Brothers Mercantile and follow the road heading southwest out of Huntsville .

Whether anybody in the slow-moving convoy looked back one last time is unknown. But it's a safe bet that some of them did. Except maybe for Margaret, who would have kept her gaze aimed at where she was going, not where she had been. She viewed her life, spent in one house or many, as merely a pilgrimage—sometimes troubled, sometimes sweet—toward what would one day be her true home.

• • •

Margaret's mother had purchased her own house in Independence several years earlier and moved there, situating what would be her final command post directly across the road from the Baptist church, her residence having quickly become something of an outer temple to what she considered the Holy of Holies.

Nearly eighty, she had increasingly become much occupied with mortality, specifically her own. She often spoke of her impending demise.

Fearing that she would be buried in an ordinary wooden box, she ordered an expensive metal coffin from New Orleans. Then she had an impressive structure of limestone, with an ornate iron gate, built beside her house to eventually be her sarcophagus, with enough room laid out beside it for her daughters' graves. Their husbands were apparently expected to find their own final resting places; she intended to end up with just her own chicks gathered close to her.[5]

The coffin arrived and was displayed prominently somewhere in her house, waiting to be put to use. The Houston children, ever adept at ruffling their grandmother's feathers and getting away with it, made much of the huge metal memento mori and teased her about it. Once, when she laid down in it to make sure she would be comfortable for eternity, she got stuck. When Sam Jr. discovered her predicament, quite the brouhaha erupted and a family legend was born that would find its way through every new generation.[6]

The Houstons had purchased their own Independence property in 1853. A log house was set back from the main road that led out of town, with a spring, a good orchard, and several hundred acres of meadow and timberland.[7] The new Baylor College for women was just across the road; the men's campus, not far away. Each had preparatory academies that the Houston children could attend.

The town itself lay between the two colleges on their hilltops. The children could walk to school every morning, and the Houston farm was close enough to the Baptist church for the family to either walk or ride the short distance to attend services. Houston liked the simple order of worship there—fewer shouted testimonials and less pulpit slapping—more than he had the more enthusiastic ceremonies in Huntsville.[8] Since Margaret's mother's house was as close as the church, she and Houston could step over in the evenings and have a cup of coffee and a visit before bedtime.

Now, with Huntsville behind them and living on their Independence farm for good, it turned out that the shepherding Houston had mentioned would be done by Sam *Secundus*, not Sam *Primus*. In an effort to provide the fifteen-year-old a practicum in taking on responsibility and seeing a project through to its conclusion, Houston bought three hundred sheep that his son was expected to tend, fatten up, and finally sell at market.

It would be a test, something of a rite of passage, to determine if the boy had the necessary resourcefulness and discipline to take on a task and see it through. Houston either forgot or conveniently overlooked the fact that he, at about the same age, had bolted from such expectations and run off to the wilderness and the Indians. He might have half expected him to fail at the task or get swindled at the sale, thus providing a valuable life lesson. But as it turned out, Sam Jr. drove his plumped, healthy herd to Galveston and turned a handsome profit.[9]

That success story, coupled with Houston's need of ready cash, might have been one of the catalysts that caused him to pack the family up yet again—the Houstons had apparently become completely portable on demand[10]—and move them to their tract of land at Cedar Point. There he—more rightly Joseph and his minions—could undertake the raising of sheep in earnest and not have far to transport them for sale.

On his way back to Washington Houston made a side trip to New York City to make a last visit to friends there and to consult an architect about having plans drawn up for a new addition to the Cedar Point house, which Houston stipulated should include one room big enough to accommodate two pianos.[11] Until the modifications were made, the family would have to make do with the only slightly improved little cabin that Margaret, a new bride, had christened Ben Lomond in 1840.

It would be a new life for everyone, and Houston, nearing his final return to Texas, seemed positively giddy about it. In a letter to Margaret dated January 21, 1859, he vowed yet again to put his old life forever behind him and submit to "petticoat government." He went on to say that he anticipated "in our rude home (for rude it must be for a while) more pleasure in one month than we have experienced for years since our union. I can . . . and will throw off the care of politics, for I cannot control them."[12] It's not difficult to imagine the reaction of his wife, so long accustomed to his nature and his best intentions, when reading that.

• • •

In Washington Houston rose from his desk and his whittling to make several final speeches in the Senate in the first months of 1859. He moved to abolish the Eastern Judicial District of Texas and attach it to the Western District, his reason being that the judge of the Eastern District, John Charles Watrous, was corrupt. Judge Watrous had long been suspected, and often accused, of fraudulent land speculations, handing down unjustly favorable sentences where cronies were involved and various other improprieties. Even though Watrous had never been found guilty of anything, Houston saw him as a troublesome fly in the ointment of justice and suggested combining the two districts would solve the problem by plucking him out and being done with him.[13]

More than a few Texas newspapers that had long been opposed to anything Houston did or stood for, themselves fed up with Watrous's behavior, condescended to praise Houston for his address. "The speech of the Honorable Senator," the *Dallas Herald* proclaimed, "is as admirable for its boldness, as it is convincing in its conclusions. In protecting the interests of his state against the grasping and defiant spirit of judicial misrule, the fearless and eloquent Senator has given indications of patriotism, which his people must gratefully appreciate, and which the country will number among its best examples of true moral heroism."[14] Such acclaim must have been bitter crow for the press to swallow, given its collective and consistent criticism of Houston. In the end, the speech brought no official action but did provide a bit of glory for the old senator to ride out on.

In the waning days of the session he spoke at considerable length in defense of his actions before and during the Battle of San Jacinto, refuting old allegations freshly arisen. Four years earlier, in 1855, David Burnet and Mirabeau Lamar, two of Houston's most zealous enemies, had published a scathing review of a new book titled *The Life of Sam Houston: The Only Authentic Memoir of Him Ever Published*, which they suspected had been penned by Houston himself and not C. E. Lester, whose name was on the cover. Their joint appraisal—probably written by Lamar, whose flowery language comes through even in its most venomous sections—was more an indictment of Houston's character than an analysis of the book, which they brushed off as "a large and noxious crop of Houston lies." Lobbing a cannonball over the bow of the Houston legend, they called the book's subject a "demagogue" and "an isolated, heartless egotist."[15]

After condemning his fraternization with Indians, his marriage to one, and even his fondness of dressing like one, Burnet and Lamar dredged up Houston's drinking, his bouts of anger and, especially, his behavior in 1836. While the Alamo was under siege, they wrote, the army's "besotted chief" was "sitting in the grog shops" at Washington-on-the-Brazos. The famous wound he received at San Jacinto had actually been minor, they believed, and "would not have disturbed the presence of mind of a brave man."[16] In fact, Burnet had been so unimpressed in 1836 by that wound, which had actually shattered Houston's ankle, that he, as president of the interim government, had denied him passage on a Texas Navy ship to New Orleans to have it operated on.

In his final Senate speech Houston gave his own account of the battle and the weeks leading up to it, repudiating all the slanders of Burnet, Lamar, and others who had fallen in with them. At the end of that address, the text of which filled thirty typeset pages, he told his colleagues that it would be the last they would hear from him: "Mr. President," he said, facing whoever was sitting in the grand chair under the scarlet canopy, "I know the high and important duties that devolve upon senators. . . . My prayers will remain with them, that light, knowledge, wisdom, and patriotism may guide them." Being who he was, he couldn't resist adding his hope that the perpetuity of the Union be "secured to the latest posterity."[17]

Also being who he was, it must have come as no surprise to senators that they had not, in fact, heard the last of him. The next day during deliberations on a post office bill, he couldn't resist rising to his feet and putting his two cents in, demanding that the El Paso–San Diego route not be scuttled in any consideration of extended mail service.[18] He left town a week later, on March 10, starting on the long road home that he had traveled so often over the years.

A snippet ran in the Washington *Evening Star* the next day, reporting that Houston "left Washington yesterday afternoon for his home in Texas. Up to the hour of his departure his rooms were crowded by his friends calling to take leave of him. No other public man ever made more, or more sincere friends here, nor was severance of a gentleman's connection with American public affairs ever more seriously regretted than in his case."[19]

During his thirteen years in the Senate he had, at times, been vindictive, trite, mean-spirited, and tactless. But at other times he had ascended to the very highest ideals set forth by the Founding Fathers and by common decency. As an orator he was no Webster, but he was at least as fine as and perhaps better than Clay and Calhoun. He had packed the galleries when he spoke, and some of his carefully chosen phrases—penned by himself, not a speechwriter—have rung nicely through history.

His manner could sometimes be called crude, his apparel often unconventional, his language coarse, and his ego verging on hubris (surely few public figures, other than perhaps Lincoln, had their pictures taken more often in those early days of photography). But never, on any day or any occasion, could his total devotion to the Union and to Texas be called into question. Nor did he ever let a decision be swayed by public opinion, political gain, or personal advantage.

He would never return to the nation's capital. Once he arrived in Texas, he would never again leave.

Eighteen

Home at last Houston settled in with the family at Cedar Point, for all appearances an old soldier finally returned from his wars who, like Tennyson's Ulysses, found himself with little more to do than sit and gaze out at "dark broad seas."[1] Several days before he left Washington, he posted a letter to Margaret in which he again proclaimed his intention to make his family his only priority henceforth: "I have thrown all other ambition to the Dogs. I learn from Texas, that there is a general wish that I should again enter into the arena of Texas politics. I am poor, but Texas can't buy my services. I would not as I have said give one smile of yours, for all the domain of Texas, but what I already own! Cedar Point!!!!"[2]

Reporters from various newspapers had themselves floated over from Galveston to get a quote or two from the old warrior and statesman now in his dotage—he was sixty-six—and in what he professed was his retirement. All of them would have asked the obvious question regarding the upcoming election; all of them would have been denied an answer.

The Texas Democrats held their convention on May 2 and nominated Governor Hardin Runnels for a second term, probably with considerable reluctance. Since his defeat of Houston two years earlier, Runnels had never lived up to his billing. His crusade to reopen Texas ports to the slave trade had been met with cold disinterest even in his own party. His failure to provide protection for settlers from Indian attacks on the western frontiers and his nearly slobbering demands for secession from the Union had made him unpopular by the time the Democrats tapped him again as their nominee, likely because they would lose face by dumping him.

The prospect of another two years of Runnels propelled an abundance of letters across the bay to Cedar Point, all of them encouraging Houston to make a second run at the governorship. Margaret, well accustomed by then to the standard protocol, would have watched him traverse through its necessary stages—surprise, indifference, refusal, doubt, contemplation, deeper contemplation, finally the request for guidance from a clutch of valued friends, their concurrence a foregone conclusion—before she accepted his completely predictable decision as one more stop on the journey.

He had as much as prophesied it himself when he told her after his defeat in the previous election to "wait till 1859." But this time he would do it on his own terms. This time around he would sit back and let the incentive come from the people themselves, one of the fundamental tenets of the Jacksonian creed. Then, should the trumpet's call sound loud and clear, he would run as an independent again, letting his own good name and record be the only flags he would march under. This time he would forgo an extensive campaign, trusting the people themselves, not assembled in any convention, to take him or leave him, giving the electorate the impression that it was of little consequence to him. Other than the 1857 campaign, the only one in which he had suffered defeat, he had always managed to make any political aspiration look like somebody else's idea.

Unsolicited, the groundswell of encouragement came, much of it from publications that had railed against him two years before and had long persecuted him for his voting record in the Senate.[3] Nothing so alters the mood of voters than the lackluster, disappointing performance of an office holder, especially one they had voted for. And the mood of a large percentage of Texans had changed drastically. In 1857 Runnels's vitriolic attacks on the Union and his fire-eater secessionist speeches had played well with an electorate that was considerably riled up, but now many Texans wanted a return to some sort of normalcy. A true Texas hero, whatever they perceived as his faults during his time in Washington, proved more palatable than another stretch of more of the same. Support for Houston was strong, to be sure, but even if it hadn't been, the time was ripe for voters' opposition to an incumbent to outweigh any doubts about his opponent.

After enough time had passed to make it obvious that the people were calling, Houston made a grand total of one campaign speech in one town, as opposed to more than forty in that many communities in the last election. The lone address was in Nacogdoches, on July 9, a Saturday. A big crowd gathered to hear him, though there is no record of free barbecue having been provided.

He started off by owning up to having been given a "regular drubbing" in the last election. "You beat me to the best style, as you had a right to do." He blamed the defeat, or at least part of it, on his having voted against the Nebraska bill in the Senate. "Well that is past," he said, probably waving it away with his hand.[4] "I was the only extreme Southern Senator who voted against it," he proclaimed, "and for that you whipped me like a cur dog. If

I was wrong, I own it and take it all back, and if you were wrong I forgive you. So we will start even again."[5]

Then, his rapt audience feeling either forgiven or forgiving—either way worked to the crafty speaker's advantage—he moved on to the various failures and missteps of his opponent. Here, he had a vast variety from which to choose. The frontier was unprotected from Comanche raids, the state's finances were a mess, and with dark clouds of an impending civil war looming on the horizon, it was hardly productive for the leader of the state to beckon them closer.

Once done with the litany of Runnels's shortcomings, Houston addressed a new idea that had slowly evolved in Texas: the creation of a state university. Apparently Runnels supported it. While in favor of common public education, though having availed himself of very little of it himself, Houston maintained that Texas couldn't yet afford to bankroll a college. Church-supported schools were fine with him, and he had served on the board of one, Austin College in Huntsville. But he warned the Nacogdoches gathering that "a great national or state [school] becomes a receptacle of the sons of politicians and the wealthy," implying that scores of bright, more deserving young men could never hope to go there. He was convinced, he said, that "unless Providence stamps a man of genius . . . education will not give it to him."[6]

In short, he believed the most valuable and dependable education came from experience, hard work, and sheer determination, entirely confident that he stood living proof of it. He summarized his opposition to building what he feared would be an elitist playground for spoiled scions in typical Houston straightforwardness: "You cannot convert a puddle duck into an eagle. You can make an educated fool, but you cannot educate a fool into a man of genius."[7]

The heart and soul of his speech was the reaffirmation of his long-held belief that a representative of the people should emerge directly from the will of the people themselves. "At their call," he said, "I have quit my flocks and herds"—here perhaps comparing himself to Cincinnatus, who had famously put down his plow to save Rome—"and am ready again to throw all my energies into the scale of the common weal."[8]

In classic Houston fashion, he managed to make it almost sound like he would rather not have the job at all. His candidacy, he reminded the throng, had not arisen from any convention of politicians, like the one that had recently nominated Runnels for a second term. "If conventions be democracy," he wondered, "how was it that democracy existed before conventions? Jefferson did glorious work for the people before their time. He was not nominated by one." As to the official agendas, the platforms that conventions generated, he maintained that "when they are used to blind the people to the designs of men [platforms] are dangerous." At that moment, as if decreed by providence, a section of the stage fell apart, tumbling several men sitting on it to the ground. "There," Houston said, pointing to the fellows getting to their feet and dusting themselves off, "did I not tell you platforms are dangerous?"[9]

• • •

The text of the speech was printed verbatim in virtually every paper in the state. Two months later Sam Houston defeated Hardin Runnels by nearly ten thousand votes, becoming the seventh governor of Texas and the only man in American history to be elected governor in two states, a distinction he still holds.

Nineteen

In mid-October 1859 while the Houstons, having returned to Independence from Cedar Point, were making ready to move to Austin for Houston's December inauguration, a disturbance in northeastern Virginia caught the nation's complete attention for three days, fanning the flames of impending war that were already burning vigorously. At twilight on a Sunday evening John Brown, a fervent abolitionist who believed the only effective way to combat slavery was to take up arms against its practitioners, led a group of eighteen men, including two of his sons, in a raid on a federal arsenal at Harpers Ferry, in what is now the state of West Virginia.[1]

Their intention was to steal the munitions, giving them the firepower needed to establish a mountain stronghold from which they could make raids on slaveholders, bringing the liberated slaves into their army. Federal forces commanded by Brevet Colonel Robert E. Lee, sent on the mission while in Virginia on leave from his army duties in Texas, surrounded the firehouse next to the armory where Brown, his men, and some hostages they had taken from the town were holed up. Brown was wounded in the attack; several others were killed.

Brown, well guarded in a secure jail, was no longer a threat. But his failed actions elevated him to the status of hero and martyr for many in the North, including numerous influential luminaries like venerable New Englanders Ralph Waldo Emerson and Henry David Thoreau. In the South Brown was generally perceived as something altogether different. Many southerners, already half afraid that their slaves might revolt, now had what they considered good reason to think that northern interlopers, inspired by John Brown's example, would help them do it.[2]

The rippling effect of the Harpers Ferry confrontation sent profoundly different messages to different places and effectively drove the sharpest wedge yet between the two sections of a nation that was already teetering on the brink of separation. John Brown was hanged on the second day of December. A week later Sam and Margaret Houston and their entourage rolled into Austin, a town Houston already disliked, to face a legislature that was, almost to a man, opposed to him and to govern a state that, once again, was hungry for war.

• • •

During the journey Margaret, who had long suffered from chronic asthma, held a handkerchief over her mouth and nose as her yellow buggy clattered through dry, floating dust. She spent her first night in Austin sitting in a chair, fearful that if she lay down, she would suffocate. That afternoon Jeff had raked up enough autumn leaves to fill several tubs; he and Eliza kept them burning in the fireplace through the night to help Margaret breathe easier.[3]

Her husband's first days in town couldn't have been pleasant either. Though the people of Texas had elected him—the returns from settlers in the west, desperate for more troops to fight Indians, had been particularly helpful—he faced an uphill battle in Austin. Support for the governor-elect was conspicuously absent in the legislature, the press, and an abundance of citizens who remembered only too well the Archives War and Houston's old, disparaging remarks about their city.

He made his first official decision even before he was officially the governor. Instead of taking the oath of office in the chamber of the House of Representatives before a handpicked audience, he made it known he intended to be sworn in and deliver his inaugural address outside, in front of the main entrance of the Capitol, which looked down a long hill, where everyone could hear it who chose to listen.

Governor Runnels, combative to the very last, was of another opinion. So, on December 21, a select group gathered in the House Chamber, per Runnels's insistence, to hear his closing remarks as governor. Then the assembly moved outside and joined a larger crowd beneath the piazza where Houston took the oath on the sunny, windy day.[4] Margaret stood nervously beside him, not having appeared in public in any official capacity in many years.

The inaugural speech was brief, barely fifteen minutes. In it Houston mentioned wanting better relations with Mexico, not mentioning that it might require an invasion to bring them about, and he talked of the need for improvements in transportation—more railroads and deeper dredging of rivers—and "improvement and perfection of the common schools." He even alluded to the possibility of a state university, but at "some future day."[5] Two decades would pass before the first buildings of the University of Texas would be erected just up the road from where he was standing.

His strongest and most carefully aimed punch came almost as an afterthought. Texas, he reminded his listeners, had in 1845 entered "not into the North, nor into the South, but into the Union."[6] With that the gauntlet was tossed.

• • •

The Governor's Mansion, across the street from the Capitol, had been built with a portion of the funds received from the federal government in the Compromise of 1850. It was a tall, stately affair built of yellow bricks and fronted by six imposing white Greek columns. The house and its yard were surrounded by a white picket fence, similar to Margaret's in Huntsville. But she probably had no illusions, when she stepped for the first time up to its ornate gate and looked up at the grand edifice on its slight hill, about this one keeping the world out as effectively as that one had.

The rooms in the mansion were enormous compared to the various rooms she had spent her life in, and the ceilings considerably higher, seventeen feet downstairs and thirteen feet upstairs.[7] An elegant stairwell curved its way up from the entryway to the upper floor, offering a much more leisurely, sweeping assent than the steep, narrow steps at Woodland her children had noisily bounded constantly up and down.

Legislative funding for proper furnishings for the house had been held up since its construction in 1856, perhaps due to the cost of construction. The first occupants, Governor and Mrs. Elisha Pease, probably used their own furniture, and Hardin Runnels, a bachelor, made do with things trundled over from the nearby little dwelling that served as the President's House during the first days of the republic. A Houston supporter in the legislature, knowing that the new first family had lived in smaller homes and wouldn't have enough things to fill this much larger one, had recently suggested that new furniture should finally be provided.

Giving voice to the overwhelmingly collective mood of the legislature regarding the newly elected governor, one member responded by saying that the state shouldn't have to purchase fancy new things for Sam Houston, who was used to "living in Wigwams." Then a debate ensued in the House of Representatives over whether or not its chamber should be used for an inaugural ball.[8]

The fete was held—in the Capitol, in the House Chamber, or elsewhere. Several copies of official invitations, brittle and faded, still survive in archives throughout the state, one of which is maintained by the Daughters of the Republic of Texas. Topped by a descending eagle printed on thick paper, the names of nearly forty "managers" are given, men who, if not all adamant Houston supporters, were at least agreeable to having their names put on the list. One of them was Samuel Augustus Maverick, whose last name would later become synonymous with both an unbranded cow and a stubbornly independent person. Disregarding a state law, he steadfastly refused to brand his cattle, figuring he knew which ones were his and that was good enough.[9]

After the inauguration and its festivities the first family retreated to their new home and commenced the celebration of Christmas. Since Houston had been absent for that holiday for years, always making his way toward Washington for the next Senate term, it was a time to cherish and enjoy. But, in the midst of her joy—both spiritual and secular—Margaret perhaps had mixed emotions. Beyond the trimmed tree with its festive twinkling candles and her gathered family, the dark night outside the windows might have reminded her that they were in a place where they were not wanted and where she did not want them to be.

• • •

The new governor launched himself into a spate of feverish activity in the first days of 1860. After delivering Sam Jr. to Bastrop, some thirty miles away, to a military academy and accepting the commandant's invitation to inspect the cadets and the firearms, he sent an urgent message to Washington demanding the government settle differences, apparently through new treaties or honoring old ones, with the Comanches and Kiowas who were misbehaving on the western frontier.[10]

Then he turned his attention to a problem in the other direction, a bandito named Juan Cortina, who had long led raids and wreaked havoc along the southern Texas border and so detested northerners that he was once heard to say that "the sight of an American makes me feel like eating little kids."[11] The desperado was hailed as a folk hero by many in northern Mexico but deemed a dangerous threat by Texans living along the Rio Grande.[12]

Legendary Texas Ranger John Salmon "Rip" Ford, a seasoned veteran of dealing with Cortina, believed that in addition to conducting his campaign of terror and agitation, the bandit sought to do nothing less than recapture Texas for Mexico.[13] He had started with one town. Shouting "Death to the Americans" and "Viva Mexico," he had recently moved his band of outlaws north, capturing the Texas town of Brownsville and hoisting the Mexican flag, giving every indication that he intended to reclaim at least that part of the old Coahuila y Tejas for his homeland. Cortina soon established a regular little kingdom, appointing himself sovereign.[14]

But not for long. Governor Houston, who had his own designs on redrawing the southern border of his state—significantly different from Cortina's plan—sent down a contingent of Rangers, where they joined federal troops in quickly defeating the Cortina mob in a skirmish at Rio Grande City. Rip Ford, a part of that force, was delighted to help deliver a measure of comeuppance to the outlaw whom he would later describe as not seeming to have "a very well-defined idea of the rights of property."[15]

By late March Washington apparently had not sufficiently responded to the governor's request regarding the Plains Indians, so he took matters into his own hands, creating seven companies of Rangers, five hundred men, to protect settlers. He also granted permission to every county judge in the region to form local militias to supplement that force.[16]

Even though the Cortina troubles were apparently over, Houston still had Mexico on his mind. He held out some hope, though perhaps very little, that the protectorate proposal he had tried to push through the Senate still had a chance of being resurrected. Suspecting it did not, he sought possible aid from an unlikely quarter.

Robert E. Lee of Virginia—son of a Revolutionary War hero, alumnus of West Point (having graduated second in his class with 1,966.5 points of a possible 2000 in conduct and perfect marks in artillery and tactics, without a single demerit[17]) and later superintendent of the academy, husband of the great-granddaughter of George and Martha Washington, and a veteran of the Mexican War in the 1840s—had recently led the assault on John Brown and his followers at Harpers Ferry while on leave in Virginia from his command with the cavalry in Texas.[18] Then he led the expedition to the border, along with Houston's Rangers, that mopped up the Cortina insurrection.[19]

Houston sent two envoys out to Colonel Lee at his West Texas fort to ascertain if he might be disposed to help mollify Mexico, implying, of course, that he lead forces to bring to fruition Houston's old grand conquest scheme. As straight an arrow as they came—that long, stainless pedigree had been meticulously earned—it hadn't taken Lee long to send his answer back to the man he probably didn't care for in the first place. In the Senate Houston had been incessantly critical of West Point, had fought vigorously against increasing the size of the army, and had specifically criticized the cavalry training that Lee oversaw.[20]

"I have no doubt," the colonel began, enunciating his response clearly so that it could not be misunderstood, and folding in a nearly hidden warning, "that arrangements will be made to maintain the rights and peace of Texas, and I hope in conformity with the Constitution and laws of the country."[21] Scratching Lee off his list, Houston fired off a tirade to Secretary of War John B. Floyd in Washington, falling just short of threatening to invade Mexico himself.[22]

Finally, the steam taken out of his old plan at every turn, the governor seems to have dropped any hopes for a conquest south of the border, at least for the time being. He turned his attention to attempting to make some sense of the state's finances, a Herculean task at best. And he made something of an effort to work with legislators who were not inclined to return the favor.

One of his children didn't help bridge relations between his father and the legislature when he held the Senate captive for a time. Six-year-old Andrew Jackson Houston, showing early signs of being as free-spirited as his older sister Nannie and as self-assured as their father, often presented himself in the office of Major E. W. Cave, the secretary of state, where he was given pencil and paper and sat himself down behind a big desk and scribbled. One morning the major was either in an ill mood or was too busy to put up with the boy and told him to get along. Andrew left in a snit and, seeing a shiny key that had been left in an enormous door, he turned it, extracted it, and high-tailed it across the road.

A while later a member of the Senate, then in session, discovered they were locked in. They threw up the windows and began to call down to people on the lawn, and very soon a crowd gathered. When apprised of the situation, Governor Houston thought for a moment and asked where Andy was. When he was located, Houston got the whereabouts of the key from his son and sent somebody over to release the senators, who were hungry for their midday meal. That evening Houston told Margaret that the boy had wielded more power over his legislature than he had yet been able to.[23] In a letter to Sam Jr. at his military academy in Bastrop, he admitted to having to "keep Andrew at the office some days, as they can't manage him at home."[24]

Twenty

In any other year Houston would have been accounted better success for his early days as governor. His newly created Rangers, in league with federal troops in the West Texas forts, had subdued the Indians to such an extent that settlers felt safer. Cortina and his outlaw following had been removed from the border. And Houston had made some inroads into bringing the state's finances into line.

But this was a year when the possibility of war moved closer every week to being a foregone conclusion. And there was no doubt in anybody's mind where the governor stood on the topic of secession. As early as mid-January he had received a letter from the governor of South Carolina requesting that a set of enclosed resolutions proclaiming the rights of states to break away from the Union be submitted to the Texas legislature for its endorsement. Houston dutifully sent them over, along with a long message condemning secession as wrong on every practical and historic level.[1]

The South Carolina resolutions, distributed to all the southern states, came finally to nothing as the 1860 presidential campaign heated up. For in that much-anticipated pivotal face-off the South had every intention of claiming the right to bolt with or without permission. Houston, clinging tight to his low opinion of conventions and refusing to allow his name to be put into nomination by one, was nevertheless still viewed as a viable contender across the country. But the field of contestants was expansive and still growing.

Houston predictably refused to accept any request to run that might come from the Democratic convention scheduled to meet in Charleston in late April. He was done with Democrats, done with political parties, and coming close to being done with politics altogether. Texas Democrats, who wouldn't have considered nominating their governor even with his consent, selected a slate of six delegates to go to Charleston, where they were expected to join other southern extremists in insisting that a plank endorsing the right to own slaves in all US territories be part of the party platform.[2]

On April 21, the twenty-fourth anniversary of the Battle of San Jacinto, a group of veterans loyal to Houston assembled at the battleground and voted to endorse their old general for the presidency, publicly stating their belief that he would "arrest the growth of the spirit of disunion" in the nation.[3] If anything came of it, Houston might have figured, it would meet his criteria of having emerged from the grassroots of the electorate, bypassing a convention.

Even before the gavel pounded the Democrats to order in Charleston, the platform committee refused to include the plank regarding protection of slavery rights in the territories. The southern delegations, including the one from Texas among whom was the former governor Runnels, promptly walked out. Under their own bylaws the Democrats couldn't select a candidate without a two-thirds majority of support, so they had no choice, with so many delegates having gone home, but to adjourn and try again a few weeks later.[4] By the time they reassembled, this time in Baltimore, the bunting and flags had been taken down and the floor swept clean of cigar stubs at the Republican convention in Chicago. The odds-on favorite to win that nomination had been Senator William Seward of New York. But Springfield lawyer Abraham Lincoln, who had served a grand total of one term in the US House of Representatives, had done some calculating.

If the Democrats, when they met again, nominated frontrunner Stephen A. Douglas, then the Republicans would need to run a westerner, since Douglas was popular in that growing region, rather than a New Yorker. And since a great many names would be put in nomination at his own convention, Lincoln figured that somebody like himself, whom nobody outside his own state was likely to vote for on the first ballot, might stand a good chance—as an anti-slavery moderate—given the many votes scattered among so many nominees, on the second or third. So he wisely courted, and courted heavily, the large Illinois delegation and eventually brought them unanimously into his camp. He would later summarize his policy during the early ballots as giving "no offense to others—leave them in a good mood to come to us, if they shall be compelled to give up their first love."[5] A sufficient number of them had done just that, and Lincoln was nominated on the third ballot.

When the Democrats reconvened in Baltimore, most of the northern delegates took offense to the southerners who had walked out being readmitted, so they followed suit and walked out themselves. The remaining delegates nominated, as Lincoln predicted, Stephen Douglas, the author of the Kansas-Nebraska Act who had already squared off against Lincoln in a series of lively debates in 1858, when Lincoln had sought, and failed, to unseat Douglas from his seat in the Senate. Southern delegates, still stinging from their treatment at the first convention and not content with Douglas, split away again and nominated John C. Breckenridge of Kentucky as their own candidate.[6]

Into this hodgepodge yet another group threw in yet another hat. They styled themselves the Constitutional Unionists and chose John Bell of Tennessee as their standard-bearer over several other candidates, including Sam Houston, who came in a close second even though he had never agreed to having his name put forth in the first place.[7] He had, however, in response to the proposal made not in a convention but on a former battlefield by his old comrades at San Jacinto, agreed, for what good it might do, to let his name be placed in nomination. When considering the overcrowded pasture of men aspiring to the nation's highest office and the turbulent circumstances that would set whoever would finally attain it to a very nearly impossible task, Houston finally grew sick of the whole business.

In early August he made the official announcement that he was withdrawing his name from any roster of candidates for the presidency. In a message of just over six hundred words addressed to "Friends in the United States," the equivalent of a modern-day press release, published in the *New York Times* on August 16 and subsequently in many other papers he made his position crystal clear: "I call upon my countrymen to forget me."[8] He seemed genuinely content with his decision. In a note to Ashbel Smith he allowed that he was "as easy as an old shoe, and have come to the sage conclusion, that if the people can do without my services, I am sure that I can do without their suffrages."[9]

Pondering what might have happened is an exercise in futility. Still, the election of 1860 dangles a "what if" that is almost too enticing to avoid. If Houston had put aside his old hatred of political conventions and allowed his name to be placed in nomination by one, and if he had gained enough support to rise through the fragmented Democratic Party to face Abraham Lincoln in the general election, could he, given his sketchy popularity in the North and his "Hero of San Jacinto" image in the Southwest, have carried enough states to become the sixteenth president? Finally, if all that could have happened, and given the reality that Lincoln's election would most certainly send the South packing, it begs the biggest "what if?" of all. Could the most horrific war in the history of the United States have been avoided?

• • •

Nobody was probably happier to hear of her husband scuttling any further presidential ambitions than his wife, who was a new mother once again, hardly an uncommon occurrence in the Houston household. Temple Houston, born full of life and voice in mid-August in the Governor's Mansion, was her eighth child, and Margaret might justifiably have prayed he would be her last. An even split of four sons and four daughters must surely have seemed a good place to stop.

She was forty-one years old, and she was tired. The scant visual evidence we have from the time confirms it. Scores of photographs survive of her husband, but we have only a very few of Margaret. He liked to have his picture taken; she obviously didn't. Neither had she agreed to have her portrait painted by the artist George Allen when he had so accurately captured her mother's stern likeness back in Huntsville.

The most famous photograph of Margaret, taken about the time of her marriage, shows a beautiful girl just out of her teens sitting timidly with one small hand resting in her lap and the other on the chair's arm. Her dark hair is perfectly parted in the middle and tucked neatly into a white, tightly knotted ruffled bonnet. She's not smiling—nobody ever seems to have smiled in studio poses from that era—but her pretty mouth appears to be on the verge of it. And there's something about her fully opened eyes that hints at her being ready to get on with life and being up to the task.

Another picture, taken when she was thirty-four, shows a woman who looks years older than that, various illnesses, considerable worry, and the delivery of several children she had had to raise in her husband's absence definitely having taken their toll. But the determination in her eyes was still in place, and she was still a beauty.

Her recent pregnancy had again proved to be a difficult one, causing her to stay confined to the mansion, sending gossip rumbling though Austin that the governor's wife was standoffish and cold. Local citizens had grown used to the big house being closed up tight during the administration of Hardin Runnels, a bachelor who had no social graces to speak of, and they missed the days of Governor and Mrs. Pease, a popular couple who entertained often and maintained something of an open-door policy for visitors.[10]

The mansion was no closed fortress, however. The Houstons did entertain close friends—such as they had in Austin—from time to time, and friends of Margaret's and various wives of government officials came for tea occasionally. Tales told by ladies who gained entrance circulated about the Houston children sometimes being so loud in other rooms that Margaret and her guests had difficulty making themselves heard over the racket.

Andy, the little lad who had locked up the Senate, was almost always the major instigator of mischief, once sneaking under a table and pinning the skirts of his sister Nettie to those of one of her friends, another time sliding down the polished banister of the long staircase and landing on the floor between the governor and a guest he was speaking with in the entryway.[11]

Despite what people might have thought as they looked up at the big house from the street, it was indeed a lively place, sometimes too lively for Margaret. One afternoon the Houston daughters had several friends over, and one of them took the group though the steps of the "pigeon's wing," a new dance that was all the rage. Hearing the commotion, the governor stepped into the parlor, and in a moment he was enjoying the demonstration, perhaps even making an effort to try it himself.

Then Margaret, who had been resting upstairs, made her entrance. Placing dancing just a bit lower than liquor in her catalogue of forbidden fruits, she had to do nothing more than stand stoically and frown to bring the curtain down on the show and send her husband back to whatever he had been doing in the first place.[12]

• • •

Governor Houston spent much of his time in the last several months of 1860 stumping against secession, perhaps seeing that crusade, given the animosity he faced in the statehouse, as the only effective battle he had left to wage. In Austin in late September he told a huge audience that disunion was tantamount to treason, even if Lincoln became president. And given the fractured Democratic Party that stood against him, it seemed more and more likely he would be. "The Union is worth more than Mr. Lincoln," he told the assembly. "If Mr. Lincoln administers the government in accordance with the Constitution, our rights must be respected. If he does not, the Constitution has provided a remedy."[13] In one twelve-day stretch in October he denounced secession in seven communities: Bastrop, Independence, Navasota, Anderson, Huntsville, Danville, and Cold Spring. His official Thanksgiving proclamation included an invocation that "we may be preserved a united people, free, independent, and prosperous."[14]

Margaret constantly worried about him moving about through mobs so put out with him and standing before defiantly angry gatherings, and unarmed, though his personal secretary constantly urged him to carry a pistol. Assassination threats came occasionally from several quarters. A former Texas Ranger named Ham White, who took offense at something Houston had once said about people from his area being horse thieves, had often proclaimed that if he saw Houston, he would kill him. The opportunity finally presented itself when he was seated across the table from the governor at a meal in a boarding house in Bastrop. White popped off with a couple of insults, whereupon Houston put down his knife and fork, sat upright, and silently stared at his assailant. In a moment White hung his head and continued eating.[15]

In addition to fretting about the safety of her husband, Margaret was, like legions of mothers of young men at the time, afraid that Sam Jr., already drilling at a military school, would soon end up in the war that was obviously coming. And Andy, the prankster, had been bitten by a dog. The wound, not appearing to be serious at first, had become so infected that his doctors were considering amputation.

By Christmastime the governor was still alive, Sam Jr. had been brought home from Bastrop and the academy, and Andy was in full recovery and in possession of two healthy legs.[16]

Two more things had happened by Christmas.

Abraham Lincoln had been elected president of the United States, and South Carolina had seceded from the Union.

Twenty-One

The first weeks of 1861 found Austin—beleaguered by a bracing cold front and bursts of chilly, blowing rain[1]—full of people from all over the state, and some from other states, demanding that Houston call the legislature into session to set into motion the course of action already being taken by Mississippi, Florida, Alabama, Georgia, and Louisiana, all of which would leave the Union by the end of January. The holdup, of course, was the governor.

Ignoring the gatherings that grew larger every day outside the front gate of the mansion and the impatient legislature that sat waiting for his call across the street, he adopted the "wait and see" attitude that had made him either famous, for his calculated attack on Santa Anna, or infamous, for his hasty retreat from him prior to the battle. He was buying time, of course, hoping to somehow avoid what seemed inevitable by putting forth every reason for staying in the Union he could come up with to sway the legislators.

He told them Texas was unique among the other southern states in that it alone was on the border of another country, and not a friendly one. He told them Texas was the only southern state plagued by Indian attacks. He told them that federal aid—admittedly not enough of it so far—had become essential in providing defense in those two areas. He told them that breaking away would mean assuming the complete financial burden of that defense.[2]

Too fired up by then to deal with logic, the fire eaters moved forward like a juggernaut toward their single goal. When the legislature took matters into their own hands and planned a convention, not to be confused with an official meeting of the legislature, to consider their course of action with or without the governor's participation or consent, Houston called a special session for January 21, where he pulled one last card out of his sleeve. He would consider supporting a decision to secede, he told the combined House and Senate, only if it was made by the people of Texas and not the legislature or the convention that had been scheduled.[3]

On January 28 Houston sat quietly and watched as the convention, held in Austin, voted overwhelmingly—152 to 6—to follow the course of the other southern states. When the governor got up to leave, the presiding officer, Judge Oran M. Roberts, told him it was good to have him in attendance. Houston stood quietly for a moment, then said, not believing the words as he delivered them, that he hoped they would have "many happy days yet."[4]

On February 23, the voters of Texas, in compliance with Houston's request for a general referendum, voted 46,153 to 14,747 to endorse the decision of the convention of the previous month. Houston's attempt to encourage the legislature to once again become the independent Republic of Texas rather than join the Confederacy, thereby possibly avoiding going to war, fell on deaf ears.[5] When the convention voted to align itself with the other breakaway states, the governor protested, maintaining that the people had been asked to only consider leaving one nation, not join another one.

In the end, all was lost, as he knew it would be. He had promised to accept the will of the people, as his undying devotion to Jacksonian democracy demanded, but he was totally unprepared for the next action of the convention, perhaps aimed directly at him. Having now become the ex facto legislature, the delegates decreed that all state officials must swear an oath of loyalty to the Confederacy. George Washington Chilton was sent across the road to the mansion on the evening of March 15 to inform the governor that he must so swear with all the others at noon the following day.

Houston thanked him for the message, showed him the door, and joined his family for an unusually quiet dinner. Afterward Houston read a few verses from the big two-volume Bible, as he did every night to the family at the table and the assembled slaves who stood behind them. Then Margaret recited her usual prayers, apparently not altered for the unique circumstances, and the younger children were sent off to bed. On her way out of the dining room Nannie, then fifteen, stopped beside her father for a moment and told him not to worry. She would later remember that that night he "wrestled with his spirit as Jacob wrestled with the angel."[6]

Houston wished Margaret good night, said he didn't want to be disturbed, and made his way slowly up the long staircase. She stayed downstairs all night, surely praying, surely reading her Bible, surely looking up occasionally as her husband's footsteps, rarely ceasing, could be heard as he paced in his stocking feet in his bedroom and up and down the long hallway far above her. At dawn he came down to find her still in her chair, having gotten no more sleep than he had. "Margaret," he said, "I will never do it."[7]

• • •

Late that morning Houston walked over to the Capitol, as he did every day. He went to his first-floor office, sat behind his desk, and waited.[8] He might have looked for things in the room he wished to have removed; he might have gone through some papers that had accumulated needing the governor's attention that wouldn't matter now. More than likely he whittled.

Upstairs the convention had been called back into session and prepared to call the state officials forward to take their oaths of allegiance. Finally the moment came that everyone had been waiting for. "Sam Houston," the clerk called, the words clear as a steeple's bell in the big room.

Some delegates tuned to look toward the door. Others listened for his distinctive footfall. Most assumed he wouldn't come; a few hoped he would. Some might have feared what he would do if he did come. "Sam Houston," the clerk called again. He waited a moment.

"Sam Houston," he called one final time as the men sat completely quiet in their seats, the most perceptive of them perhaps realizing the point of no return had been reached. In short order the silence was broken as the governor's office was declared vacant, and Ed Clark, the lieutenant governor, was sworn in to fill it.[9] Though he provided no answer to the legislature and its hastily called convention to which he gave no credibility, Houston did offer one in a letter to the people of Texas.

Addressing it to "Fellow Citizens," he explained that "in the name of your rights and liberties, which I believe have been trampled upon, I refuse to take this oath." Then he trotted out his reasons in a flowing cadence: "In the name of the nationality of Texas" and of "the constitution of Texas" and finally of "my own conscience and manhood, which this convention would degrade by dragging me before it . . . I refuse to take this oath." Finally, he shared a refusal that was born of something purer and stronger than mere anger and disappointment. He felt, at the end of all of it, a cold loneliness. "I have seen patriots and statesmen of my youth one by one gathered to their fathers, and the government which they have created rent in twain, and none like them are left to unite it again. I stand the last almost of a race, who learned from their lips the lessons of human freedom."[10]

• • •

Several offers of support—not of the moral variety but involving real force and real guns—came soon thereafter, a couple of them possibly from President Lincoln. Several sources, including Marquee James's biography of Houston and Ida Tarbell's of Lincoln, concur that San Antonio merchant and postmaster George Giddings, in Washington to secure a mail route contract, was approached by Postmaster General Montgomery Blair, taken to the president, and sent back to Texas with a confidential message for Houston. Lincoln had perhaps sent a first note before this much more specific one that supposedly offered to make Houston a major general in the federal army and provide him with fifty thousand troops to keep Texas in the Union.[11]

According to Houston's slave Jeff Hamilton, recounted many years later when he was a very old man, the recently ousted governor met with four Unionist friends—James Throckmorton, William Rogers, David Culberson, and Ben Epperson—and read them the letter. All but Epperson advised against accepting the president's offer. Houston concurred, saying that if he had been twenty years younger, he would have made a different decision. Then he crumpled up the letter and tossed it in the fire, destroying any proof that it ever existed.[12]

Another offer, this time not from the president, arrived on the evening of March 19 as the family sat in the light of a single candle amid all their possessions packed and ready for transport. Several friends sat with them, one of them being Ed Sharp, Houston's plow salesman chauffeur from the 1857 campaign. Suddenly there was a loud knock on the front door of the Governor's Mansion.

Houston first assumed the armed men on his porch had come to evict him a bit earlier than expected. Then they told him they were prepared to return him to his rightful office by any means necessary. He thanked them, and told them to disperse. "My God," he said, once back inside, "is it possible that all the people have gone mad?"[13] Across the street the state flag of Texas had been brought down, and the banner of the Confederate States of America flew over the Capitol.

Twenty-Two

The next morning the same wagons and buggies that had brought the Houstons to Austin from Independence left to take them back. After a short stay with Margaret's mother they would go to their farm at Cedar Point. This time Houston claimed young Jeff as the driver of his buggy, probably sending Joshua over to Margaret in her yellow rig. Not far into the journey Houston told Jeff to drop back from the caravan and slow down a bit, adding that they were "both out of office" and didn't need to be in any hurry.[1]

During a stop in Brenham before making the last short leg of the trip, some local veterans who served under Houston in 1836 asked if he would make a public statement explaining his actions. He declined, more than once, until somebody shouted that he shouldn't be allowed to speak anyway. This was all it took for him to change his mind.

Everybody went into the courthouse, where Houston stood before the packed, noisy courtroom. Somebody shouted that he should be tossed out. Somebody yelled that he should be shot. At which point Hugh McIntyre, a local farmer and a secessionist, rose to his feet and drew a large Colt revolver, which probably looked even larger at that tense moment.

Having the audience's complete attention, he reminded them that Houston had been invited to speak. "I myself," McIntyre said, "think that Governor Houston ought to have accepted the situation, and ought to have taken the oath . . . but he thought otherwise. There is no man alive who has more right to be heard by the people of Texas. Now, fellow citizens, give him your close attention." Then he leveled his steely gaze, and perhaps his revolver, at the group of men who had been making most of the racket. "And you ruffians, keep quiet, or I will kill you."[2]

Houston didn't speak long, having nothing new to add to his already well-known warnings and arguments. Spending very little time rehashing his devotion to the Union, he reminded the crowd that the vox populi was not "always the voice of God" and warned them about the absolute inadvisability of entering the approaching conflict. He said he found "false and absurd" the secessionists' contention that "the superior courage of our people" would make them victorious over "ten times our number of Northern forces." "The civil war," he told them, "which is now near at hand will be stubborn and of long duration. The soil of our beloved South will drink deep the precious blood of our sons and brethren."[3]

He and Jeff got out of town alive, but no more popular than when they had arrived. Three weeks later southern forces fired on Fort Sumter, a federal stronghold in South Carolina, sending a declaration of war that would be impossible to misinterpret.

• • •

Still intent on raising his voice, which he believed to be one of the few voices of reason amid a clamor of fanaticism, Houston made the short trip from Cedar Point across the bay to Galveston on April 19 and stood on the second-story balcony of the Tremont Hotel to face an angry mob in the street below that was even louder and more threatening than the one in Brenham.

"Let me tell you what is coming," he thundered over the gathering. "Your fathers and husbands, your sons and brothers, will be herded at the point of the bayonet. You may, after the sacrifice of countless millions of treasure and hundreds of thousands of lives, as a bare possibility, win Southern independence . . . but I doubt it." Then he turned his attention to whom, exactly, the South would be going up against. "I tell you that, while I believe with you in the doctrine of state rights, the North is determined to preserve this Union. They are not a fiery, impulsive people as you are," he told them, looking directly down into a fiery, impulsive lot indeed, "for they live in colder climates. But when they begin to move in a given direction, they move with the steady momentum of a mighty avalanche."[4]

The crowd hadn't heard him, of course, any more than the crowd in Brenham had heard him. At some point he must have seen the folly of any further efforts at tilting public opinion. Back in Independence to check on his farm, he told an assembly that "the time has come when a man's section is his country" and that since Texas had chosen to join the Confederacy, "I can but cast my lot with theirs."[5]

All the while Sam Jr. had been pondering what his place should be in the new circumstances. He finally told his parents he was considering joining the Confederate army. Margaret, unsurprisingly, was dead set against it, Houston slightly less so. He wrote to his son that "when it is proper you shall go to war, if you really wish to do so. It is every man's duty to defend his country; and I wish my offspring to do so at the proper time and in the proper way." Apparently still holding out some hope that Texas leaders might come to their senses and break away from the Confederacy, reverting to an independent republic, he closed his note by urging patience: "We are not wanted or needed out of Texas, and we may soon be wanted and needed in Texas. Until then, my son, be content."[6]

Ultimately his advice had no more effect on his son than it did on the various crowds that had booed and threatened him. In August Sam Jr. joined the Bayland Guards in Galveston under the command of his father's old friend Ashbel Smith.[7] Houston paid to have his son's gray Confederate uniform made. Margaret supplied a small Bible that would fit conveniently in a pocket or a knapsack.[8]

• • •

Houston was now finally old, and he knew it. His war injuries gave him considerable trouble, so he used a cane all the time and sat more often than he stood. On nice days Margaret took walks with him, though they were considerably slower and shorter walks than they had once taken. More often they took rides in the buggy. At night Margaret read to him from the Bible or, at his insistence, from editors' attacks on his character in the newspapers. But there were fewer of those now. He was quickly becoming old news.[9]

He went a few times to Galveston to watch Sam Jr.'s outfit drill throughout the autumn. He came home to Margaret full of news about their boy and the precision displayed by the entire troop. Then he would find a comfortable rocker or lie down for a bit.[10] It had been only five years since he had pushed himself through all those towns in summer heat, sleeping on the ground every night, in his first campaign for the governorship. But now just a ride in a boat and standing to watch boys march was exhausting.

Christmas was a cold and wet business, with strong winter winds sending frigid spray up off the bay. Nannie, Maggie, and Mary Willie had come by stage from Independence; their grandmother stayed put, her traveling days behind her. Houston made Sam Jr. model his uniform for his sisters.[11]

On March 12 Houston leaned on his cane in Galveston and watched his oldest son ship out with his company for Missouri. The parting was courteous, succinct, and doubtlessly difficult for both of them. Houston handed Sam Jr. a few little gifts from his young brothers and sisters and the small Bible from Margaret. Then the brief ceremony ended as such things commonly end, in any era and any nation, with the father stuffing a few dollars into the son's pocket.[12] Houston watched the company's departure until it was completely out of sight before leaving.

It had been less than a year since belligerent mobs threatened him at every turn. Now he walked unnoticed and unmolested along a busy street. People had, it would seem, done exactly what he had asked them to do when he withdrew his name from any consideration for the presidency in 1860. They had forgotten him.

• • •

Margaret wouldn't be consoled. She wrote to her mother that she "could not forget that my boy, my darling . . . is gone from me, probably never to return."[13] In early May, her prediction stood a good chance of proving accurate. A letter arrived from someone identifying himself as a friend of Sam Jr.'s. He began by stating they had no doubt heard of Shiloh, which was a church near Corinth, Tennessee.[14] They had. Houston had sent a letter to Nannie a month before in Independence, in which he wrote that "we have heard of a great battle at Corinth." He said they had reason to believe that was where Sam Jr.'s company was, but no news had come to confirm it. They had their confirmation now.

The correspondent ended his brief note by telling them he had shaken hands with their son on the morning of April 7 near the battlefield. "Sam and some 7 or 8 others were in no way accounted for. . . . Some may have been wounded—and perhaps have fallen into the hands of the enemy. . . . I by no means despair of Sam's safety."[15] Margaret could only believe that her son was dead. Houston probably conceded, though silently, that it was likely so.

• • •

While Margaret prayed and wept, Houston had to keep the family going. Their only source of income at the time came from the sale of cordwood, which Joshua and his crew of other slaves chopped from the timber on Cedar Point and shipped to Galveston on barges.[16]

The city had been blanketed under a tight federal blockade since 1861, having to make do with what could be grown or produced on the island or could be slipped in by blockade runners. On a narrow finger of land surrounded by water where salt grass was much more abundant than trees firewood likely sold quickly.

One afternoon in September as Margaret was tending to her flower bed while Houston was in Galveston, she looked up to see an emaciated, crippled soldier leaning against her rail fence. She watched him for a long moment, probably wondering if he needed something to eat or if he was simply resting before moving along.

"Ma," Sam Jr. said. "I don't believe you know me."[17]

Twenty-Three

The unexpected reunion was cause for a great celebration. But, with the family in dire straits financially, the fatted calf could hardly be slain if there wasn't one. Margaret, with or without a celebration, was jubilant, giving all the credit for her son's homecoming to God. As it turned out, she had much to do with it herself.

Sam Jr. had been badly wounded in the groin at the Battle of Shiloh, just as his father had been at Horseshoe Bend in 1813. He had lain on the battlefield for all of the afternoon, bleeding badly and drifting into and out of consciousness as the Rebel army retreated. About dusk a Yankee chaplain walking by saw him move slightly. He knelt down, lifted a small Bible from his knapsack, and read "Sam Houston, Jr., from his Mother, March 5, 1862."

It so happened that this particular chaplain was one of a group of ministers who had sent a letter to Senator Houston in 1854, thanking him for voting against the Kansas-Nebraska Bill. He looked down at the young man who was obviously struggling hard to stay alive and asked if he was related to General Sam Houston of Texas, who had served in the United States Senate. "My father," was the pained reply.

The chaplain quickly located a doctor and a stretcher, and Sam Jr. received the medical attention that saved him before being sent to Camp Douglas in Illinois as a prisoner of war. In September he was taken to Vicksburg, Mississippi, in an exchange of prisoners. After a promotion to lieutenant and a short stint as an instructor of tactics it became evident that he was too frail to serve and he was discharged. Weak and undernourished, he began his long journey home.[1]

Margaret, the source of the providential Bible that had provided not one but possibly two blessings—a family story holds that the day before young Sam was wounded the little book had stopped a musket ball that would have otherwise proved fatal[2]—still refused to take any credit for what she knew was a bona fide miracle when she heard the story.

• • •

When Union forces captured Galveston in October, Houston, believing Cedar Point was too close to the island for comfort, planned to move the family once again. The logical destination would be Independence, where Sam Jr.—much improved and back in college at Baylor—two of his sisters, Margaret's mother, and a place to live awaited them.

Had the choice been hers, Margaret would have headed there.[3] But by that time her husband, nearly seventy, probably sensed the innate need that finally comes to most ramblers, given enough traveling over enough time, to go home and stay there. So he decided the family would move to Huntsville, where they had nowhere to live and no family.

After arriving in December they found that their old home, Woodland, was for sale, but Houston, who once could have bought any building in town on the strength of his name alone, couldn't arrange credit to make the purchase.[4] His stained reputation, it seems, had preceded him. So the family rented an odd structure across the road from Oakwood cemetery, Huntsville's burial ground.[5]

It was a narrow, long, wooden two-story house set in a copse of cedars and fig trees, with an impressive oak tree to provide shade over the entrance at one end.[6] Two square crenelated, flat-topped towers were stationed on either side of a steep set of steps leading up to the second-story front door. The towers, which resembled twin smokestacks on the bow of a riverboat, and narrow outside walkways with rails and balusters extending the length of the house on both levels gave the place its unavoidable name. Huntsville folk called it the Steamboat House.

It had recently been built by Rufus W. Bailey, a language professor at Austin College.[7] One story has it that he intended the strange edifice, odd even in the age of ornate structures being built and labeled Victorian, as a wedding gift for his son and his bride-to-be, who promptly refused to live in it.[8]

Though she would rather have been in her old Woodland home if she couldn't be in Independence, Margaret made the best of the situation and set about planning where crepe myrtles and flower beds would go in the spring. Her son was home from the war, growing stronger every day and back in school, and her husband had finally come out of the big world, though not as either of them would have wished it, and into only hers. Which had been her goal for a very long time.

Cold, damp winter settled on Huntsville and took up residence, sending chilly gusts through the undulating hills and smoke from chimneys into leaden skies. Houston, visibly more feeble, his shock of hair gone white, and relying on a hickory walking stick carved by Joshua, spent most of it in the little room on the ground floor behind the front stairs he had claimed as his bedroom. The steps were sufficiently steep and numerous to make any visits upstairs a rare pilgrimage.[9]

On the first day of 1863 the Confederacy won Galveston back from Union control in an early-morning surprise attack that sent soldiers in along with several cotton-clad vessels with cannons blasting down from Harrisburg to overtake federal ships in the harbor and troops on the shore.[10] Houston sent a congratulatory letter to General John B. Magruder, the recently appointed commander of Confederate forces in Texas who had planned the attack. Magruder's reply, which did not arrive until a month later, provided a bit of never-unwelcomed praise for the old warrior. "No hostile foot now treads on the soil of Texas," the general wrote, "and it gives me peculiar pleasure to announce that fact to the hero of San Jacinto."[11]

Warmer weather brought Houston out of his room under the stairs more often; with Jeff as his chauffeur he took rides in the buggy on pleasant days. With his health taking an upturn, though slight, Margaret's and his concern turned quickly to their daughter Maggie's. She had come down with scarlet fever in Independence and, too ill to continue her studies, had been brought to Huntsville to recuperate. By the time she was well enough to return to school, too much of the semester had transpired for her to do so, so she stayed home and served as her father's secretary.[12]

In late March Jeff drove Houston down to the city that was named for him to visit Eber Cave, his old secretary of state who had let young Andy scribble in his office. Cave had joined the governor in refusing to take the oath to the Confederacy and had also been removed from office.[13] During his stay, Houston was invited to give a speech. Rarely one to decline such a summons, he accepted.[14] By the time Jeff delivered him to the hall, he was exhausted. He spoke softly during the address, coming up with just enough energy at times to get the words out.

His reminder that "the days draw nigh onto me" during his opening remarks left little doubt that he realized, and so should they, that this would likely be his last trip to a podium. "I have been buffeted by the waves," he told them. "I have been borne along time's ocean until shattered and worn I approach the narrow isthmus which divides me from the sea of eternity." Even at the end he could still woo a crowd with both prose and poetry, snippets of it pilfered outright from actual poets. "Once I dreamed," he said, "of empire vast and expansive for a united people." The Unionists in the audience had, like himself, accepted the current way of things and could relate to that. To the surprise of some he pledged his support of the southern cause,[15] perhaps seeing little profit in stating yet again what he surely still believed to be the eventual outcome of the war.

But before he was done he did manage to work in a sad lament about the old days and their demise. "The dream is over," he told the audience that was no doubt straining to hear him. "The charm is broken. From one nation we have become two . . . to attest how vain were the dreams of those who believed that the Union was a thing of forever."[16]

It wasn't the last time on that trip that he would let his mind wander back to the past. On their way back to Huntsville Jeff followed his passenger's directions along a different route that took them through the San Jacinto battlefield. Houston had Jeff stop the buggy at a specific tree, where he lowered himself down painfully and sat quietly, leaning back against the trunk, for a long while. Twenty-seven years earlier he had sat in the same spot, his ankle shattered by a Mexican rifle ball, and looked up at the defeated General Santa Anna, who, having traded his general's uniform for a pair of trousers and a jacket taken from an abandoned cabin, was captured while trying to run away after the battle.[17] Jeff would later remember that Houston had "a far off look in his eyes" as he gazed out at the empty, flat place, and that his eyes were wet.[18]

Houston wrote, or dictated, his last will and testament on April 2, leaving his entire estate to Margaret. One clause was specific: "To my eldest son, Sam Houston, Jr., I bequeath my sword worn in the Battle of San Jacinto, it never to be drawn only in defense of the Constitution, the Laws, and the Liberties of his Country."[19] He made no mention of a particular country, but it's not difficult to assume which one the old Jacksonian Unionist hoped it would be. He had offered that sword or a new one as a dangled carrot when Sam Jr. had been a child, wanting him to study hard and keep his grades up. Apparently the boy had opted for the new one or had fallen short in his studies. Soon it would be his.

In May Union prisoners taken in the Battle of Galveston when their ship, the USS *Harriet Lane*, was captured, were transferred to the penitentiary down the hill from the Steamboat House. Houston had himself driven down to the prison soon after their arrival to see that they were being treated properly. Then he made several return trips to check on them, but he also enjoyed the visits. The war had emptied Huntsville of most male camaraderie, and some of the old men and young boys who were left had little use for a man they saw as a traitor to the glorious cause.[20]

Knowing that the prisoners were surely aware that their vessel had been named for a niece of President Buchanan who served as the White House hostess for her bachelor uncle during his administration, he might have told them that he had known Harriet Lane—the woman, not the ship—and had attended several state dinners she had overseen.

By June his health had again spiraled downward, enough so that Margaret felt it warranted a visit to a spa called Sour Lake, near Grand Cane, where she hoped the muddy hot mineral baths might prove beneficial.[21] He agreed to go, maybe grasping at a last straw, maybe wanting to please Margaret and settle her troubled mind.

When he returned a month later, he was in worse shape than when he had left.[22] Margaret put him to bed in his small downstairs room and sent word to Ashbel Smith, in Galveston, asking if he could come. Smith, recovered from injuries he sustained at the Battle of Shiloh on the same day Sam Jr. had been wounded, arrived a day or two later in his Confederate uniform and examined his old friend.[23]

During the last, hard days in Austin Smith had shown up at the Governor's Mansion carrying a petition with the signatures of many Galvestonians requesting that Houston call the legislature into session to consider secession. Houston had refused to see him.[24] But that didn't matter now, and their friendship was as solid has it had been when Smith was President Houston's surgeon general in the first years of the republic. Smith stayed for several days, during which time Houston's illness turned into pneumonia. Finally, Smith told Margaret there was nothing more he could do for him, bid his friend farewell, and returned to Galveston.[25]

After that Margaret rarely left Houston's bedside. She held his hand, read to him, wiped the sweat from his face, and prayed for him. Jeff sat with him through the still, stifling nights, fanning him. One night Jeff fell asleep and dropped the fan on Houston's face. Pushing the fan aside, Houston told Margaret, sitting in her chair, that he wanted the two of them to go and get some rest, that there was "no use in both of you breaking yourselves down."[26]

Several men came up from town, bringing with them Reverend Samuel McKinney, who had once been the president of Austin College and had recently moved back to Huntsville. One of the men, Major Carothers, asked Houston what he intended to do with Jeff, who was obviously so devoted to him that he wouldn't leave his side. Houston told him he had already freed all his slaves.[27] He might have thought he had.

The previous October Houston, having read the text of President Lincoln's Emancipation Proclamation stating that all slaves in states still in rebellion would be freed on the first day of 1863, sent Joshua to gather all his slaves under the shade of the big oak and read the document to them from the steep front steps of the house. When he finished, he told them he and Margaret didn't wish to wait until January and were setting them all free immediately.

Jeff claimed much later to remember the episode in great detail, down to and including what Houston was wearing—his best Sunday suit (perhaps only because it was a Sunday)—and Eliza's moaning and swaying, believing that Yankee soldiers would come collect her and take her away from Margaret and the family.[28] She finally hushed when Margaret assured her they would never be separated,[29] and Houston told the little congregation that they could stay if they wished and he would pay them for as long as he could.

Jeff recalled that the total quiet that followed Houston's address was one of the most solemn moments he had ever known and that Margaret and the smaller children, all of the slaves, and very nearly Houston himself were crying. Joshua was the first to announce, past a lump in his throat, that he was "going right on working" as usual, and only a few others chose to leave.[30]

It's a touching scenario, and there is little reason to doubt that it occurred. But it's important to note that the family bond and trust described by Jeff as an old man were almost certainly not shared by all in attendance that day. Elsewhere Jeff recalled that most slaves thought constantly of ways to escape or eventually purchase their freedom, though he claimed to have never considered either.[31]

Houston's grand gesture, while perhaps well intended and sincere, accomplished nothing. The Texas Constitution, freshly revised and quickly adopted when Texas joined the Confederacy, expressly forbade the emancipation of slaves by their owners.[32] Houston might not have been aware of it, but that is unlikely since he apparently read every newspaper he could find. Perhaps his long-held allegiance to the Union negated, in his mind, the hugger-mugger contrivances of the legislature once it joined the Confederacy. Or maybe, as some have suggested, he performed his public manumission just for show, suspecting the Union, as he had so often predicted, would eventually win the war and it would be a moot point. The will that he had recently signed stipulated that his slaves—a total of a dozen valued at $10,530.20—were to be left to Margaret.[33] Whatever his reasoning or his reason, he could feel confident, on what was obviously his deathbed, that Jeff, slave or free, would be cared for. Margaret would see to that.

McKinney, a Presbyterian minister, asked Houston how he stood with the Lord. "All is well," he told him, barely loud enough to be heard. "All is well."[34] Then he went back to sleep. Late the next afternoon, on Sunday, July 26, all the Houston children except Sam Jr. were in the little room listening to their mother read from the Bible. Their father had drifted into and out of consciousness all day. Suddenly he moved a bit, and Margaret stopped her reading and leaned down close to him. He managed to whisper "Texas," once, and then, after a brief hesitation, again. A short moment later, while his wife held his hand in hers and their children stood weeping around them, he breathed out one final thought: "Margaret." Then he was gone.[35]

• • •

His funeral was a small event, held the next day directly above the little room in which he died, in the parlor of the Steamboat House. Every straight-back chair in the house was placed facing the casket that had been built recently in the prison by the ship's carpenter of the *Harriet Lane*.[36] The Baptist preacher was out of town, so Margaret had to make do with the pastor of the Presbyterians, Reverend James Cochran.[37]

Margaret had written a poem and asked the minister to read it at the service. Her life with Houston had begun with one of her poems—"To a Withered Pink," an ode to the flower he had placed in her hair on their first meeting when they gazed at their star of destiny—so it was fitting that she said good-bye to him with this one, which she titled "To My Husband." In the final stanza she voiced the hope that she had long held:

And now may peace, within thy breast,
From him descend, and there remain!
Each night oh mayst thou sweetly rest,
And feel thou hast not liv'd in vain.[38]

After the final prayer the coffin was maneuvered down the steep steps by pallbearers who were Houston's fellow Masons and carried in a steadily falling summer rain across the muddy road to the cemetery. He was buried at the far end, in a place he had chosen himself just a few feet from the grave of his friend Henderson Yoakum.

Neither ceremony was attended by many people, possibly because of the small room in which the funeral had been held and the rain that fell on the burial.[39] But it's unlikely that many more would have shown up in a big church on a sunny day. In the midst of the war, and given the low regard in which so many held him, many papers wouldn't have wasted space needed for war news and casualty lists on even a tiny notice of his death. In the grip of the federal embargo, it's possible that no one in Washington, where he had been a household name for so long, would learn that he was gone until after the war.

That night after his burial, when everyone had left and her children were in bed, Margaret dipped the nib of her pen into her small inkpot and made a short entry in the family Bible: "Died on the 26th of July," she wrote, in the same delicate, precise script with which she had penned all the letters to her husband over the years, "Genl Sam Houston, the beloved and affectionate husband, father, devoted patriot, the fearless soldier—the meek and lowly Christian."[40]

• • •

The gravestone that would be placed sometime later was a modest one, nothing more than an upright tablet with his name and dates of his birth and death. A much larger, ornate monument would be dedicated there on April 21, 1911, the seventy-fifth anniversary of the Battle of San Jacinto, with state and federal officials in attendance. William Jennings Bryan, the unsuccessful Democratic candidate for the presidency in the last three elections, gave one of the speeches. That bigger, grander monument, the work of Italian sculptor Pompeo Coppini, boasts an impressive relief portrait of General Houston on horseback. On either side are winged, toga-clad figures symbolizing Victory and History.

Fourteen years later, in 1925, an impressive statue of the general—again on horseback; again by an Italian, Enrico Filiberto Cerrachio—was lowered onto a massive granite arc in the city named for Houston. Thc general's horse, Saracen, has one front hoof raised and his handsome head lowered. His rider's outstretched hand points determinedly toward San Jacinto as he looks back toward the little army he beckons to follow him.

Then, in 1994, a colossal effigy of Houston purported to be the world's largest statue of an American hero was erected just south of Huntsville on a pine-covered knoll overlooking the freeway that links the cities of Houston and Dallas. Texas sculptor David Adickes's Houston, thirty tons of concrete and steel, soars sixty-seven feet above its ten-foot-tall base.

At the bottom of the marker on the general's grave a quote attributed to Andrew Jackson is chiseled into the Texas granite between two laurel wreaths: "The world will take care of Houston's fame."

It took the world an awfully long time to get around to doing it.

Twenty-Four

Margaret, though more than twenty years younger than her husband, might have felt that her life's work was complete when she buried him, except that she had a houseful of children, several of whom were very young. Still, she had a difficult time facing life without him, causing her older children to be concerned about the depths to which her grief had plunged her.[1] It was the one occasion in her life, it seems, that her faith might have faltered, offering no clear path forward.

In autumn she made the last of her many moves, relocating the family in Independence, where she bought a house close to her mother's. Eliza went with her, of course, and Jeff. It wouldn't have occurred to either of them to do anything other than go wherever Margaret went. She left Joshua in Huntsville, knowing he could earn his living as a blacksmith.

After the war ended, Joshua came to see Margaret and, knowing what her financial situation must be, laid a leather bag on the table between them. He told her it contained two thousand dollars that he had saved, in United States gold coins, not Confederate script. He told her he wanted her to have every penny of it.

She was so moved that she had to wait a moment before speaking. Then she told him she couldn't accept the gift, as generous and thoughtful as it was. She wanted him, she said, to use that money as General Houston would have wanted him to, in securing good educations for his children.[2] And he did.

Joshua, who took Houston as his last name, became a successful businessman, city alderman, and county commissioner in Huntsville. His son became a college professor. Joshua died in 1902 and was buried in Huntsville's Oakwood cemetery, a few yards from Sam Houston's grave.[3]

Margaret's health never improved to any considerable degree. In December 1867 she contracted yellow fever and died during an epidemic of the disease that swept the state. She outlived her husband by four years and her mother, Nancy Lea, by three.[4] Though her family and friends were saddened by their loss, they had absolutely no doubt where this final journey would take Margaret, knowing no one more deserving of her destination.

Nannie, married by then, took her youngest siblings in and raised them. Eliza probably didn't ask to go along but simply gathered her things and climbed into whatever vehicle was making the trip.

After Margaret's death Jeff married and worked in several jobs in Independence before moving to Belton, where the Baylor women's college had moved when the men's college relocated in Waco. Jeff worked as a janitor at the school, now named Mary Hardin Baylor, for many years before retiring.

Sam Houston had never been able to follow through on his intention to purchase Jeff's mother and siblings, for the man he bought Jeff from had quickly sold them off to several other people. Jeff finally located his mother and visited her a quarter century after their tearful separation hours before Houston had stepped into his life and changed it forever. Jeff lived in Belton until he died, in 1941, within two months of his hundredth birthday.

• • •

Because the bodies of yellow fever victims were not allowed to be transported and had to be interred immediately, Margaret was buried not in Huntsville but in a hastily dug grave beside her mother's imposing sepulcher housing its metal coffin in Independence.[5]

There, across the street from the site of the Baptist church they had so loved, mother and daughter rest beside one more member of the family, who had grown up with Margaret and come to Texas with her. The third tombstone, put up in 1898 by the Houston children, bears an inscription with no last name. But a heartfelt title precedes the first: "Aunt Eliza" the stone reads.

Twenty-Five

In 1941 another Senator Houston rose to his feet and made a motion in Washington.

Andrew Jackson Houston, almost eighty-eight years old, had been appointed by Texas governor "Pappy" Lee O'Daniel to complete the remaining few months of the term of recently deceased Senator Morris Shepherd.[1]

Governor O'Daniel, a colorful character even by Texas standards who launched his political career via the popular weekly radio show he hosted featuring a country swing band called the Light Crust Doughboys, had been the president of the Burris Mill and Elevator Company, the show's sponsor, whose most popular product was Light Crust Flour.[2] "Pass the biscuits, Pappy!"—a constant catchphrase on the hokey program—could easily have translated for listeners, legions of them, into "Pass Pappy into the Governor's Mansion!"

They had done so. Now that his term was drawing to a close, he had his eye on the Senate seat for himself, and he needed a stopgap replacement who wouldn't run against him at the end of the session. Houston fit the bill perfectly. He was sufficiently old and ill to make his not launching a campaign virtually a lead-pipe cinch. And his direct link to the family whose name was synonymous with Texas—he was Sam and Margaret's only surviving child—would make his appointment a popular choice among voters and be a feather in O'Daniel's cap.

Since he had locked the Texas Senate in their own chamber at the age of six, Andrew had been a lawyer, a district clerk, and an unsuccessful candidate for governor. In 1898 he put together one of the several groups of volunteers for Teddy Roosevelt's Rough Riders—not including himself on the roster—and four years later was rewarded for his efforts by being named US marshal for East Texas by Roosevelt, by then the president. Sometime in the 1930s Houston became the honorary superintendent of the park on the site of the Battle of San Jacinto.

When he accepted Governor O'Daniels's appointment, many doubted, given his age, condition, and the brevity of the unexpired term, that he would ever set foot in the Capitol. He surprised them. He showed up for at least one committee meeting and pushed legislation through to provide funding in the amount of $250,000 to finish paying for the monument on the San Jacinto battlefield, a 567-foot-tall obelisk with an observation deck under a mammoth lone star perched on top, which had been built between 1936 and 1939.[3]

Then he died, a little over two months after his appointment. O'Daniel did indeed succeed him to fill the Senate seat until 1949, when Congressman Lyndon Johnson won it and rode it into history.

• • •

Andrew's brothers and sisters also left their stamps on Texas, each in his or her own way. Sam Houston Jr., who died in 1894, attended medical school after the Civil War and practiced in Belton, Waco, and other places before marrying in 1875. When his wife died eleven years later, he moved to Independence and spent the rest of his days writing and publishing short stories. It's interesting to imagine what his father, having forbidden his oldest son to read novels and write poetry, would have thought of that.

Nannie, the second born, fully lived up to her mother's early prediction that she would be a "perfect romp." When she was nineteen and everyone expected her to marry, she proclaimed that she would never consider it until she found a man who could afford to pay the preacher fifty dollars and take her to Niagara Falls on her honeymoon. At twenty she found one. After her marriage to Joseph Styles Morrow, a successful businessman, the newlyweds settled, after the requisite jaunt to Niagara Falls, in Georgetown, just north of Austin. When her mother died in 1867 Nannie brought her youngest brothers and sisters into her home and raised them, along with six children of her own. At the time of her death in 1920 at the age of seventy-four, Nannie was a much-loved pillar of society in Georgetown, where she is buried.

Maggie, named of course for her mother, fell in love at seventeen with a Baylor College student who was a boarder at her grandmother's house in Independence. After living for a while on a farm not far away, they moved into her mother's old house, where they raised five children. When her husband died, Maggie moved to San Antonio in 1904, where she quickly established herself as a patron of the arts. The transplanted German artist Elisabet Ney became a great friend and visited her often. When Maggie died in 1906, the flag at the Alamo was lowered to half-mast and bells tolled throughout San Antonio in her honor.

In 1850, when Sam Houston was in Washington fighting for the compromise bill, everyone had been expecting the fourth Houston child to be a boy, to be named after Andrew Jackson. Mary William Houston, called Mollie, surprised them. After graduating from Baylor Women's Seminary, Mollie moved in with Nannie and her younger siblings in Georgetown, where she met and married Nannie's husband's cousin John Simeon Morrow in 1871. The couple later moved to Abilene, where John opened a law office. After his death Mollie became the postmistress of Abilene in 1910. She died in 1931 at the age of eighty-one.

The fifth Houston child, and the fourth girl in a row, was named for her mother's sister. Antoinette Power Houston inherited her mother's literary talent, becoming a published poet. One of her poems, "The Flag of a Single Star," was put to music and sung by schoolchildren throughout Texas. In 1877, Antoinette married William Lorraine Bringhurst, a college professor, at the Governor's Mansion in Austin. Governor Richard B. Hubbard gave the bride away. The couple eventually moved to the new Texas Agricultural and Mechanical College near Bryan (the name would be later truncated to Texas A&M). Bringhurst was the first doctor of philosophy at the school and served for a while as the institution's interim president.

After moving to San Antonio with her family, Antoinette became an active member and official historian of the Daughters of the Republic of Texas. Who could have possibly produced better credentials? One day in the Alamo, which was maintained as the shrine of Texas liberty by Antoinette's organization, she ran her hand along the surface of a table that had belonged to her parents. A visitor cautioned her not to lean on it, as it was a souvenir of General Sam Houston.

"So am I," she told him. Antoinette was killed in a car accident in 1932 at the age of eighty. Her funeral was held in the Alamo.

William Rogers Houston, the frail Willie that his mother had described to his father as a "pale little cripple" when he was an infant, grew up in the Georgetown household of his sister Nannie. After college he served for many years as an agent in the Indian Service of the Department of the Interior, an agency dedicated to providing assistance to Native Americans, a life's work that would have greatly pleased his father. In 1920 Willie, at the age of sixty-two, suffered an apparent heart attack and fell from his horse while riding to an Indian reservation in Oklahoma. His death occurred just two months before the death of his sister Nannie, who had raised him. He never married.

The eighth and last of the bunch, Temple Lea Houston, had the distinction of being the first child born in the Texas Governor's Mansion. He was not yet three when his father died in Huntsville and only seven when he lost his mother. He, too, was raised by his sister Nannie. Temple became a colorful, eccentric, and consistently successful trial lawyer who was well known throughout the entire Southwest, counting gunslingers and cattle thieves among his clients. Such was his fame that he was elected to two terms in the Texas Senate.

Of all he children he came closest, by all accounts, to exhibiting the colorful, reckless nature of his father when he had been a daring young soldier and adventure seeker, before Margaret tamed him. Temple died in 1905, survived by his wife and four children.[4]

• • •

When US Senator Andrew Jackson Houston passed away in 1941, 101 years after the marriage of his parents, all of the brood were finally gone, leaving enough offspring to virtually ensure that Sam's and Margaret's descendants will roam Texas for a very long time.

Perhaps forever.

Epilogue

During a visit in the summer of 1917 to the State Capitol—a sprawling, impressive edifice of pink granite that amplifies the legendary Texas swagger and ego by being the largest of any American statehouse, pushing its massive dome up several feet higher than that of the national Capitol in Washington—a petite lady of nearly sixty noticed something that caught her attention.

Ellen Maury Slayden was in Austin with a friend to attend the impeachment trial of Texas governor James "Pa" Ferguson for a potpourri of alleged infractions. The proceedings attracted a multitude—governors didn't get impeached every day—and Ellen Slayden might have found the close quarters a mite stuffy and wanted some space. Or maybe she needed to visit the ladies' lavatory. Whatever her reason, she noticed something odd as she wandered around the huge building.

That night she recorded it in the current volume of the diary she had kept religiously every day since she and her husband, James Luther Slayden, had moved to Washington in 1897 for his first of eleven terms as a US congressman.

In the early 1960s Slayden's diary, which she had condensed and edited shortly before her death in 1926, would come into the hands of the fiancée of Walter Prescott Webb, one of the titans of Texas historians. He read it, found it fascinating, was instrumental in finding a publisher for it, and eventually wrote its introduction.

Washington Wife: Journal of Ellen Maury Slayden from 1897–1919 has proved to be one of the best chronicles we have of Washington society in general and the colorful and intriguing assortment of government leaders from the era of President McKinley and the Spanish-American conflict to that of Woodrow Wilson and World War I, all of it delivered in the keen, witty, and often acerbic voice of a uniquely perceptive onlooker. Of Teddy Roosevelt she wrote, "The President has innumerable relatives. . . . Some of them are so tacky that it really makes me like him better to see how frankly he parades them on occasions."[1]

What caught her attention on that day in the State Capitol in 1917 was a large oil portrait of Sam Houston outfitted in ancient Roman attire.

Noticing that it had been moved, perhaps more than once, from where she had previously seen it, she wrote that the picture of Houston, "undressed and clutching anxiously at a slipping toga, has gotten as far in its demotion as the rear of the press gallery, so near the door that I hope he will escape to the bathroom."[2] Slayden's dislike of the painting is apparent, but her entry also—intended or not—serves well as a metaphor of the Houston legend and legacy slipping further and further into the mist, at least on the national and international levels.

In 1916, a year before Slayden's discovery, historian Emerson David Fete had all but overlooked Houston entirely in his *History of the United States*, published in New York by Henry Holt and Company. After a ludicrously succinct account of the birth of Texas—a total of four sentences encapsulating the conflict between settlers and Mexico, the fall of the Alamo, the Declaration of Independence, and the Battle of San Jacinto—Houston is mentioned only once in the entire volume, as having been made president of the new republic.

Eventually many of the numerous books about Houston that are still in print migrated to the section in bookstores designated as "Regional" or "Texana," where he doesn't belong. His stamp is on every inch of the western United States. And his almost unbelievable résumé—commanding general of an army of liberation, twice the president of a republic, US senator, governor of two states—is unparalleled by anyone in American history. The city named for him is one of the largest in the nation. And his last name was the first word spoken by a human being, from the lunar landing module, on the surface of the moon.

He had his flaws, of course, and plenty of them. He had a mean streak. Though an onslaught of criticism, much of it scathing, was constantly hurled at him, he gave as good as he got. He tended to ridicule and belittle, in public and private, those opposed to him, and apparently enjoyed doing it. Still, when juxtaposed with all the dirt digging and mudslinging that constantly transpires in the modern political arena, his behavior seems mild.

Houston's efforts on behalf of American Indians and his defense of their inherent rights are counterbalanced by his unwavering support of the institution of slavery. Even given the apparent fact that he treated his own slaves fairly and with kindness and considering that slavery was accepted by many in his era and his society as a necessity, it's difficult to fathom how a man so devoted to justice and human rights could have missed the opportunity to rail against the practice.

News anchor and author Dan Rather, a graduate of the university in Huntsville named for the general, put the enigma perfectly: "It's worth asking ourselves," Rather writes, "how Sam Houston 'got it' in his dealings with the Cherokee and didn't 'get it' in his dealings with the African Americans around him."[3] It's a fair question. Obviously the "lessons of human freedom" he once claimed to have learned from the lips of patriots and statesmen of his youth did not apply, for him, to all humans.[4]

• • •

When Houston was a young man, before Andrew Jackson and Margaret Lea got hold of him, his deficiencies, misbehavior, and missteps would have made him the unlikeliest of potential heroes. But history has, every so often, provided a few people—cometh the hour, cometh the man—to do some amazingly great and important thing, often at the cost of significant personal sacrifice. Sam Houston was one of those people, particularly so on a dark night in the Texas Governor's Mansion in 1861 when he reached the moment that would define him.

His star was bright and persistent as it traveled over Texas and the western United States in the nineteenth century, casting its light far beyond those places and that era. And it shined the brightest, in one brilliant burst of light, at the very end of its journey.

Author's Notes and Acknowledgments

It was during a fall semester a long time ago, while the signature on my high school diploma was still wet, that I watched wide eyed as two students almost came to fisticuffs in the American history class that was one of my first college courses. The pair spewed out their arguments like floodgates opened wide. The topic was the Vietnam War. One was for it and the other was not, not an uncommon disagreement in 1970, especially on university campuses.

The defender of the war was big on honor and sacrifice and pride. The other fellow said that he was in favor of those things too, but his argument rested on his belief that there ought to be better ways to settle differences than sending young men off to be killed. Then he turned to the rest of us in the class—thirty or so kids in a ground floor corner classroom of Old Main, one of the oldest college buildings in Texas—and challenged us to rise up and protest the war. He invoked the usual litany of great takers of difficult moral stands, among them Gandhi, Thomas Beckett, and the recently assassinated Martin Luther King Jr. He even, I think, threw in Atticus Finch from *To Kill a Mockingbird.*

The professor let the battle continue until time to dismiss us, all the while wiping his glasses with a big handkerchief by an open window. Then he thanked the two for their "lively discussion." Somebody asked whom he thought was right. He put his glasses back on, slid his notes and a couple of books into his leather satchel, and clamped it shut. "Hell if I know," he said, which fetched some nervous laughter. "But our young devotee of Gandhi needn't look so far away for a role model. This very institution is named after one that fits the bill."

"Why him?" somebody asked.

He smiled. "Take a Texas history class and find out." More laughter. The professor let it drift away. Then he looked at his wristwatch, dismissed us, and we all drifted away.

A few minutes later I walked past the old Austin College building that had been built up the hill from the Houstons' favorite home, Woodland, in 1850. At the university bookstore down another long hill—flat land is hard to come by in Huntsville—I bought a used copy of *The Raven,*

Marquis James's Pulitzer Prize–winning 1929 biography of Houston. That night I found a hero.

I spent so much time in the museum across the street from the college that the staff probably grew tired of me. I made the hour and a half drive down to San Jacinto, where I wandered around, map in hand, on the flat terrain where his ragtag little army won Texas' independence.

I would sit on of the benches in the museum's pretty park and imagine the old boy puttering around Woodland, preserved intact just across a pond skirted by slowly gliding ducks and geese (the Steamboat House, where he died, was moved across town from its original location in 1936, the centennial of Texas Independence, to sit close by the Woodland home), or sitting in a rocker in the open dog run in the middle of the house, leaning on his ever-present walking stick. In my conjuring I watched him in his final years—Tennyson's "idle king" home finally from his wars and adventures if ever there was one. I brought him fully to life when I looked over at where many of the last scenes of his extraordinary journey took place, like the final moments of the final act of a particularly compelling play.

Nearly a half century later, my fascination with and respect for Houston hasn't diminished. In fact, getting older has allowed me to know him better and, in at least one regard, to respect him more. When I was writing about his extensive 1857 campaign speaking tour with the plow salesman Ed Sharp—rattling into all those towns in that hot summer in a two-horse buggy, sleeping on the ground most nights—I was almost exactly the age Houston was at the time. After a couple of those days and nights I suspect I would have canceled the rest of the excursion and headed for the comforts of home.

The opportunity to read Houston's and Margaret's letters—they wrote a plethora of letters—and to rummage through the account ledgers at Gibbs Brothers Mercantile, to walk through the rooms in Woodland and the Steamboat House and gaze out their windows at a time far removed from the modern world has been an amazing and completely gratifying experience. It was as close to actual time traveling as I'm likely to get.

In the early 1920s Carl Sandburg, just completing his research for the first volume of his monumental biography of Lincoln, penned these lines of what he might have intended to become a poem, which was never published: "I say you dead are more real than people I see on streetcars, in offices and restaurants, in parks and cigar store hangouts."[1]

Having spent so much time with the Houstons and other denizens of their world, I know exactly what Sandburg meant. It was an honor and a privilege to have traveled with them for a while.

• • •

Each source I consulted proved to be informative, but several quickly became essential.

James Haley's *Sam Houston*, the most comprehensive and thoroughly documented of the biographies, was my constant "go-to" and the final arbitrator when several chroniclers disagreed on some point. Other constant companions were Marquis James's *The Raven*, the single book that first brought me to Houston; Randolph B. Campbell's *Sam Houston and the American Southwest*; and Marshall De Bruhl's *The Sword of San Jacinto: A Life of Sam Houston.*

Llerena Friend's *Sam Houston, the Great Designer* provided a valuable insight into Houston's Senate career and particularly his ability to pursue two or more objectives at the same time, often playing one against the other.

For elements of the story involving Margaret I went most often to William Seales's *Sam Houston's Wife* and for her marriage to *Star of Destiny: The Private Life of Sam and Margaret Houston* by the Houstons' great-great-granddaughter Madge Thornall Roberts. For the whirlwind of events leading up to San Jacinto and its immediate aftermath I turned to H. W. Brands's fine *Lone Star Nation.*

First-person narratives written by contemporaries of Houston—especially Noah Smithwick, Rip Ford, William Ballaert, Henderson Yoakum, and Melinda Rankin—were tremendously helpful with descriptions of that unique era and sprawling landscape.

Finally, the compilation of the many letters exchanged between Sam and Margaret, carefully edited by Madge Thornall Roberts and filling four fat volumes, provided perhaps the most indispensable resource of all. In those missives the bond shared by those two incredible people comes through in every line, chronicling a relationship based on love, respect, and mutual admiration that rivaled that of John and Abigail Adams.

Enormous debts of gratitude are due to many people, and it would be a great error to suggest that this book could have ever reached completion without their kind assistance.

This is my second project with Logan Kibodeaux, research associate extraordinaire, and I truly hope it is not the last. Logan's knowledge of the history of the United States and especially of Texas, the Southwest, and the American Civil War is vast, and his penchant for accuracy was beyond helpful. I must have seemed a dense pupil to him at times; I appreciate his patience and, above all, his friendship.

Mac Woodward—great- (several times) grandson of Houston's friend Henderson Yoakum and a descendant of Huntsville's Gibbs family, and himself the director of the Sam Houston Memorial Museum in Huntsville and, at the time of my research and writing, the mayor of Huntsville—took all my calls, even well past the point that I was embarrassed placing them, and answered all my questions. The museum, the finest compendium of Houston archives and artifacts in existence, opened its doors to Logan and me and allowed us to wander into rooms of the Houstons' homes, Woodland and the Steamboat House, and sort through documents that most people never have access to. Mac and his archivists Michael Sproat and Sandra Rogers were knowledge and generosity personified, and their museum is a true American treasure.

Other archives and collections at Washington-on-the-Brazos, Brenham, San Jacinto, and in Huntsville at the offices of Gibbs Brothers and the Thomason Special Collections Room at the Library of Sam Houston State University were also beneficial.

Once again I find myself in debt to my old college roommate Jim Willett, the director of the Texas Prison Museum, for his knowledge of the history of the Walls, the state penitentiary where Houston visited Union prisoners captured in the Battle of Galveston.

Jay Dew, Gayla Christensen, Patricia Clabaugh, Christine Brown, and others at Texas A&M University Press were wonderful to work with and supportive through the entire process, as were copyeditor Cynthia Lindlof and my longtime friend and literary agent Jacques de Spoelberch.

As always I'm grateful to Karen, my compass, best friend, and constant sounding board through many wonderful years and ten books. All of the glowing accolades that Sam Houston bestowed in his abundant letters on his good wife are equally applicable to mine.

To all, many thanks. Any mistakes in the narrative are completely mine, not theirs.

Ron Rozelle
Lake Jackson
January 2017

Notes

PROLOGUE

1. James L. Haley, *Sam Houston* (Norman: University of Oklahoma Press, 2002), 400.

2. Jeff Hamilton and Lenoie Hunt, *My Master: the Inside Story of Sam Houston and His Times* (Austin: State House Press, 1992), 85.

3. Donald R. Walker, "Texas State Penitentiary at Huntsville," *Handbook of Texas Online*, http://www.tshaonline.org/handbook/online/articles/jjt01, uploaded on June 15, 2010, published by the Texas State Historical Association.

4. Ibid.

5. Haley, *Sam Houston*, 408.

6. Alan Dean Lehmann, "Trapped in Texas" (master's thesis, Sam Houston State University, 1995), 19.

7. T. R. Fehrenbach, *Lone Star: A History of Texas and the Texans* (New York: American Legacy Press, 1983), 357.

8. Haley, *Sam Houston*, 8.

9. Madge Thornall Roberts, *Star of Destiny: The Private Life of Sam and Margaret Houston* (Denton: University of North Texas Press, 2001), 3.

10. Randolph B. Campbell, *Sam Houston and the American Southwest* (New York: HarperCollins, 1993), 3.

11. Ibid., 4.

12. M. K. Wisehart, *Sam Houston: American Giant* (Washington, DC: Robert B. Luce, 1962), 4.

13. John Hoyt Williams, *Sam Houston: The Life and Times of the Liberator of Texas, an Authentic American Hero* (New York: Touchstone, 1993), 27.

14. Marshall De Bruhl, *The Sword of San Jacinto: A Life of Sam Houston* (New York: Random House, 1993), 35.

15. Campbell, *Sam Houston*, 5.

16. Arthur Wylie, *The Life and Times of Sam Houston*, Sec. 2, "Ancestry and Youth" (1855; repr., Raleigh, NC: LuLu Press, 2014), 9–10.

17. De Bruhl, *Sword of San Jacinto*, 38.

18. Haley, *Sam Houston*, 74.

19. De Bruhl, *Sword of San Jacinto*, 125.

20. Campbell, *Sam Houston*, 30.

21. Marquis James, *The Raven: A Biography of Sam Houston* (Austin: University of Texas Press, 1988), 165.

22. H. W. Brands, *Andrew Jackson: His Life and Times* (New York: Random House / Anchor, 2005), 508.

23. De Bruhl, *Sword of San Jacinto*, 134.

24. Llerena Friend, *Sam Houston, the Great Designer* (Austin: University of Texas Press, 1954), 164.

25. James, *The Raven*, 182.

26. Williams, *Sam Houston*, 99.

27. De Bruhl, *Sword of San Jacinto*, 142; James, *The Raven*, 186; Haley, *Sam Houston*, 91.

28. Haley, *Sam Houston*, 104.

29. George Brown Tindall and David E. Shi, *America: A Narrative History* (New York: W. W. Norton, 1992), 527.

30. Paul D. Lack, "Consultation," *Handbook of Texas Online*, http://www.tshaonline.org/handbook/online/articles/mjc08, uploaded on June 12, 2010, published by the Texas State Historical Association.

31. Friend, *Sam Houston*, 67.

32. H. W. Brands, *Lone Star Nation: How a Ragged Army of Volunteers Won the Battle for Texas Independence and Changed America* (New York: Doubleday, 2004), 282.

33. Rupert Richardson and Adrian Anderson, *Texas: The Lone Star State* (Englewood Cliffs, NJ: Prentice Hall, 1993), 98.

34. Sue Flanagan, *Sam Houston's Texas* (Austin: University of Texas Press, 1964), 177.

CHAPTER 1

1. Madge Thornall Roberts, ed., *The Personal Correspondence of Sam Houston*, 4 vols. (Denton: University of North Texas Press, 1999), 3:123.

2. Ibid., 124.

3. Haley, *Sam Houston*, 327.

4. William Seale, *Sam Houston's Wife: A Biography of Margaret Lea Houston* (Norman: University of Oklahoma Press, 1970), 80–81.

5. Ibid., 81.

6. Roberts, *Personal Correspondence*, 3:124.

CHAPTER 2

1. Seale, *Sam Houston's Wife*, xv.

2. James, *The Raven*, 257.

3. Friend, *Sam Houston*, 72.

4. Seale, *Sam Houston's Wife*, xvi.

5. Ibid.

6. Roberts, *Star of Destiny*, 3.

7. Ibid., 17.

8. Ibid., 18.

9. Haley, *Sam Houston*, 212.

10. Wisehart, *Sam Houston*, 339.

11. Haley, *Sam Houston*, 312.

12. Wisehart, *Sam Houston*, 344.

13. Roberts, *Personal Correspondence*, 1:3n.

14. Ibid., 2.
15. Ibid.
16 Wisehart, *Sam Houston*, 343.
17. Roberts, *Star of Destiny*, 19–20.
18. De Bruhl, *Sword of San Jacinto*, 266.
19. Seale, *Sam Houston's Wife*, 13.
20. Friend, *Sam Houston*, 79.
21. Charles A. Spain Jr., "Flags of Texas." *Handbook of Texas Online*, http://www.tshaonline.org/handbook/online/articles/msf01, uploaded on June 12, 2010, modified on November 28, 2016, published by the Texas State Historical Association.
22. Haley, *Sam Houston*, 214.
23. Andrew Burstein, *The Passions of Andrew Jackson* (New York: Knopf, 2003), 144.
24. Brands, *Andrew Jackson*, 198.
25. John Salmon Ford, *Rip Ford's Texas* (Austin: University of Texas Press, 1987), 29.
26. Campbell, *Sam Houston*, 88.
27. Ibid., 87.
28. Haley, *Sam Houston*, 215.
29. Roberts, *Star of Destiny*, 26.
30. Ibid.
31. Haley, *Sam Houston*, 218.
32. Roberts, *Personal Correspondence*, 3:127.

CHAPTER 3

1. De Bruhl, *Sword of San Jacinto*, 320.
2. Williams, *Sam Houston*, 43.
3. De Bruhl, *Sword of San Jacinto*, 60.
4. John C. Calhoun, "Speech on the Oregon Bill," in *Union and Liberty: The Political Philosophy of John C. Calhoun*, ed. Ross M. Lence (Indianapolis: Liberty Fund, 1992), http://teachingamericanhistory.org/library/document/oregon-bill-speech/.
5. Haley, *Sam Houston*, 301.
6. William Carey Crane, *Life and Select Literary Remains of Sam Houston of Texas* (Dallas: W. G. Scarff, 1884), 201.
7. Holman Hamilton, *Prologue to Conflict: The Crisis and Compromise of 1850* (Lexington: University Press of Kentucky, 2005), 52.
8. Sam Houston, *The Writings of Sam Houston, 1813–1863*, ed. Amelia W. Williams and Eugene C. Barker (Austin: University of Texas Press, 1938–43), 5:95–107.
9. Roberts, *Personal Correspondence*, 3:130.

CHAPTER 4

1. Patricia Prather and Jane Monday, *From Slave to Statesman: The Legacy of Joshua Houston* (Denton: University of North Texas Press, 1995), 9.

2. Seale, *Sam Houston's Wife*, 80.

3. Ibid., 39.

4. Ibid., 262.

5. De Bruhl, *Sword of San Jacinto*, 301.

6. Seale, *Sam Houston's Wife*, 97.

7. Prather and Monday, *From Slave to Statesman*, 22.

8. Seale, *Sam Houston's Wife*, 97.

9. Haley, *Sam Houston*, 293.

10. Seale, *Sam Houston's Wife*, 125.

11. Prather and Monday, *From Slave to Statesman*, 36.

12. De Bruhl, *Sword of San Jacinto*, 68.

13. Roberts, *Star of Destiny*, 100.

14. Roberts, *Personal Correspondence*, 2:231.

15. Michael Sproat (curator of collections, Sam Houston Memorial Library), interview with author, 2015.

16. Prather and Monday, *From Slave to Statesman*, 36.

17. Kay Bailey Hutchison, *Unflinching Courage: Pioneering Women Who Shaped Texas* (New York: Harper, 2013), 185.

18. Frannie Bush Leigh, "Recollections," Sam Houston Memorial Library Manuscript Collection, Huntsville.

19. Roberts, *Personal Correspondence*, 1:2.

CHAPTER 5

1. Seale, *Sam Houston's Wife*, 80.

2. Ibid.

3. Roberts, *Star of Destiny*, 112.

4. Roberts, *Personal Correspondence*, 3:143.

5. Ibid.

6. Ibid., 146.

7. Ibid.

CHAPTER 6

1. Charles L. Dwyer and Gerald L. Holder, "Huntsville, Texas," *Handbook of Texas Online*, http://www.tshaonline.org/handbook/online/articles/heh03, uploaded on June 15, 2010, published by the Texas State Historical Association.

2. Donald R. Walker, *A Frontier Texas Mercantile: The History of Gibbs Brothers and Company, Huntsville, 1841–1940* (Huntsville: Texas Review Press, 1997), xx.

3. William Bollaert, *William Bollaert's Texas* (Norman: University of Oklahoma Press, 1989), 284.

4. Ibid., 285.

5. Noah Smithwick, *The Evolution of a State: Recollections of Old Texas Days* (Austin: University of Texas Press, 1983), 233.

6. Ford, *Rip Ford's Texas*, 15.

7. Seale, *Sam Houston's Wife*, 135.

8. Prather and Monday, *From Slave to Statesman*, 44.

9. Walker, *Frontier Texas Mercantile*, 8.

10. Ibid.

11. Ibid., 10.

12. Gibbs Mercantile ledgers, Sam Houston Memorial Museum archives, Huntsville.

13. Walker, *Frontier Texas Mercantile*, 21.

14. Mary S. Estill, *Vision Realized: A History of Sam Houston State University* (Huntsville, TX: Sam Houston State University Press, 1970), 2.

15. James Willett (director of the Texas Prison Museum), interview with author, 2015.

16. Seymour V. Connor, "Rankin, Melinda," *Handbook of Texas Online*, http://www.tshaonline.org/handbook/online/articles/fra39, uploaded on June 15, 2010, published by the Texas State Historical Association.

17. Ibid.

18. Melinda Rankin, *Texas in 1850* (Boston: Damrell & Moore, 1850), 15.

19. Ibid., 16.

20. Ibid., 138.

21. Ibid., 142.

22. Ibid., 138.

CHAPTER 7

1. Clifton Daniel, "1850," in *Chronicle of America* (New York: Simon & Schuster, 1989), 338–39.

2. Roberts, *Personal Correspondence*, 3:69.

3. Ibid., 74.

4. Ibid., 154.

5. Ibid., 143.

6. Ibid., 158.

7. Wisehart, *Sam Houston*, 533.

8. Lonnelle Aikman, *We the People: The Story of the United States Capitol* (Washington: US Capitol Historical Society, 1993), 41.

9. Friend, *Sam Houston*, 202.

10. Edwin P. Hoyt, *Zachary Taylor* (Chicago: Reilly & Lee, 1966), 149.

11. Sam Houston, "Speech on the Subject of Compromise, Feb. 8, 1850," in Houston, *Writings*, 5:119–44.

CHAPTER 8

1. Seale, *Sam Houston's Wife*, 150.

2. Crescent Dragonwagen, *The Cornbread Gospel* (New York: Workman, 2007), 10.

3. Elizabeth Silverthorne, *Plantation Life in Texas* (College Station: Texas A&M University Press, 1986), 106.

4. Haley, *Sam Houston*, 305.

5. Friend, *Sam Houston*, 203.

6. Danielle Brissette, "Slavery in the Houston Household," *Sam Houston Memorial Museum Blog*, December 28, 2012, http://samhoustonmemorialmuseum.blogspot.com/2012/12/slavery-in-houston-household.html.

7. Houston, *Writings*, 4:211.

8. Donald Braider, *Solitary Star: A Biography of Sam Houston* (New York: G. P. Putnam's Sons, 1974), 228.

9. Brands, *Andrew Jackson*, 558.

10. Roberts, *Personal Correspondence*, 3:137.

11. Ibid., 160.

12. Ibid.

CHAPTER 9

1. Roberts, *Personal Correspondence*, 3:167.

2. Ibid., 168

3. James, *The Raven*, 423.

4. Haley, *Sam Houston*, 306.

5. Roberts, *Personal Correspondence*, 3:168–69.

6. Ibid., 170–71.

7. Ibid., 173n.

8. Ibid., 172.

9. Ibid., 173–74.

10. Ibid., 174–75.

11. Ibid., 176.

12. Ibid., 176–77.

13. Ibid., 179.

14. William Shakespeare, *Hamlet, Prince of Denmark*, Folger Shakespeare Library ed. (New York: Washington Square Press, 1992), 209, act IV, scene 5, lines 83–84.

15. Roberts, *Personal Correspondence*, 3:178.

CHAPTER 10

1. Roberts, *Personal Correspondence*, 3:179.

2. John C. Waugh, *On the Brink of Civil War: The Compromise of 1850 and How It Changed the Course of American History* (New York: Rowman & Littlefield, 2003), 75.

3. Ibid., 19.

4. Walker Lewis, *Speak for Yourself, Daniel: A Life of Webster in His Own Words* (New York: Houghton Mifflin, 1969), 394.

5. Isaac Asimov, *Our Federal Union: The United States from 1816 to 1865* (Boston: Houghton Mifflin, 1975), 122.

6. Robert C. Byrd, *The Senate, 1789–1989: Classic Speeches, 1830–1993* (Washington, DC: Government Printing Office, 1994).

7. Daniel Webster, "Speech of the Honorable Daniel Webster, on the Compromise Bill: Delivered in the Senate of the United States, on the 17th Day of July, 1850," HathiTrust Digital Library, https://catalog.hathitrust.org/Record/101715726.

8. S. P. Lyman, *Life and Memorials of Dan. Webster*, vol. 2 (Appleton, MN: Appleton Press, 1855), http://www.ebooksread.com/authors-eng/s-p-samuel-p-lyman/life-and-memorials-of-daniel-webster-volume-2-amy.shtml, 157.

9. John Shaw, *JFK in the Senate: Pathway to the Presidency* (New York: St. Martin's Press, 2013), 158.

10. Lyman, *Life and Memorials of Dan. Webster*, 155.

11. Webster, "Speech of the Honorable Daniel Webster."

12. Tindall and Shi, *America*, 600.

13. John Greenleaf Whittier, "Ichabod," in *The Norton Anthology of American Literature*, shorter 4th ed. (New York: W. W. Norton, 1979), 637.

14. Stephen Vincent Benet, "The Devil and Daniel Webster," in *Selected Works of Stephen Vincent Benet*, vol. 2, *Prose* (New York: Farrar & Rinehart, 1942), 39.

15. Ibid., 32.

16. Priscilla Myers Benham, "Rusk, Thomas Jefferson," *Handbook of Texas Online*, http://www.tshaonline.org/handbook/online/articles/fru16, uploaded on June 15, 2010, modified on July 18, 2016, published by the Texas State Historical Association.

17. Houston, *Writings*, 5:145–47.

18. Wisehart, *Sam Houston*, 548.

19. Seale, *Sam Houston's Wife*, 136.

20. Friend, *Sam Houston*, 205.

21. Ibid.

CHAPTER 11

1. Roberts, *Personal Correspondence*, 3:182.

2. Seale, *Sam Houston's Wife*, 138.

3. Ibid., 144–45.

4. James, *The Raven*, 423.

5. Walter M. Woodward, "Henderson Yoakum, Texas Historian" (master's thesis, Sam Houston State University, 1994), 68.

6. Roberts, *Star of Destiny*, 205.

7. Seale, *Sam Houston's Wife*, 151.

8. Wisehart, *Sam Houston*, 536.
9. Roberts, *Star of Destiny*, 214.
10. Seale, *Sam Houston's Wife*, 148.
11. Roberts, *Star of Destiny*, 219.
12. Ibid., 220.
13. Roberts, *Personal Correspondence*, 2:52.

CHAPTER 12

1. Seale, *Sam Houston's Wife*, 152.
2. Roberts, *Star of Destiny*, 219.
3. Seale, *Sam Houston's Wife*, 153.
4. Les Standford, *The Man Who Invented Christmas: How Charles Dickens's* A Christmas Carol *Rescued His Career and Revived Our Holiday Spirits* (New York: Crown, 2008), 224.
5. Roberts, *Personal Correspondence*, 3:281.

CHAPTER 13

1. Friend, *Sam Houston*, 248.
2. Ed Sharp, "Interview," reprinted in the *New York Times*, November 6, 1892.
3. Haley, *Sam Houston*, 315.
4. Ed Sharp, "Interview."
5. Haley, *Sam Houston*, 344.
6. Tindall and Shi, *America*, 610.
7. Walter M. Woodward, *Sam Houston: For Texas and the Union* (New York: Rosen Publishing Group, 2001), 87.
8. Charles Edward Lester, *The Life of Sam Houston: The Only Authentic Memoir of Him Ever Published* (New York: J. C. Derby, 1855), sec. 47, 13.
9. Houston, *Writings*, 6:444.
10. Ed Sharp, "Interview."
11. Seale, *Sam Houston's Wife*, 185.
12. Friend, *Sam Houston*, 280.
13. Roberts, *Star of Destiny*, 252.
14. Roberts, *Personal Correspondence*, 3:298.

CHAPTER 14

1. Ed Sharp, "Interview."
2. Haley, *Sam Houston*, 351.
3. Ed Sharp, "Interview."
4. Roberts, *Personal Correspondence*, 3:21.
5. Ibid., 411.
6. Ibid., 219.
7. Ibid., 7.
8. Brissette, "Slavery."

9. Prather and Monday, *From Slave to Statesman*, 2.
10. Hamilton and Hunt, *My Master*, 2.
11. Ibid., 5.
12. Ibid., 6.
13. Ibid., 7.
14. Ibid., 6–8.
15. Ibid., 9.
16. Ibid., 38–39.

CHAPTER 15

1. Ed Sharp, "Interview."
2. Ibid.
3. Haley, *Sam Houston*, 348.
4. Ibid.
5. Ibid.
6. Claudia Hazlewood, "Archive War," *Handbook of Texas Online*, http://www.tshaonline.org/handbook/online/articles/mqa02, uploaded on June 9, 2010, modified on August 26, 2016, published by the Texas State Historical Association.
7. Haley, *Sam Houston*, 350.
8. James, *The Raven*, 389.
9. Wisehart, *Sam Houston*, 572.
10. Braider, *Solitary Star*, 287.
11. Seale, *Sam Houston's Wife*, 188.

CHAPTER 16

1. Benham, "Rusk."
2. Roberts, *Personal Correspondence*, 4:263.
3. Houston, *Writings*, 6:463–66.
4. Andrew Marvell, "To His Coy Mistress" (ca. 1650), in *The New Oxford Book of English Verse, 1250–1950*, ed. Helen Gardner (New York: Oxford University Press, 1972), 334–35.
5. De Bruhl, *Sword of San Jacinto*, 373.
6. Haley, *Sam Houston*, 354.
7. Roberts, *Personal Correspondence*, 4:270.
8. Haley, *Sam Houston*, 354.
9. Friend, *Sam Houston*, 257.
10. Haley, *Sam Houston*, 354.
11. Houston, *Writings*, 7:223.
12. Miller Center of Public Affairs, University of Virginia, "James Buchanan: Foreign Affairs," US Presidents, 2017, https://millercenter.org/president/buchanan/foreign-affairs.
13. Tindall and Shi, *America*, 609.
14. Roberts, *Personal Correspondence*, 4:286.
15. Friend, *Sam Houston*, 299.

16. Roberts, *Personal Correspondence*, 4:264.
17. Ibid., 301.

CHAPTER 17

1. Seale, *Sam Houston's Wife*, 188n.
2. Haley, *Sam Houston*, 356.
3. Seale, *Sam Houston's Wife*, 161.
4. Ibid., 187.
5. Ibid., 163.
6. Ibid., 238.
7. Prather and Monday, *From Slave to Statesman*, 49.
8. Seale, *Sam Houston's Wife*, 163.
9. Haley, *Sam Houston*, 356.
10. James, *The Raven*, 385.
11. Prather and Monday, *From Slave to Statesman*, 52.
12. Houston, *Writings*, 7:218–19.
13. Friend, *Sam Houston*, 265.
14. Ibid.
15. De Bruhl, *Sword of San Jacinto*, 364.
16. Ibid., 364–65.
17. Houston, *Writings*, 7:306–35.
18. Friend, *Sam Houston*, 268.
19. Williams, *Sam Houston*, 312.

CHAPTER 18

1. Alfred, Lord Tennyson, "Ulysses" (1833), in *The Norton Anthology of English Literature: The Major Authors*, 6th ed., ed. M. H. Abrams (New York: W. W. Norton, 1962), 1891–93, line 45.
2. Roberts, *Personal Correspondence*, 4:347.
3. Braider, *Solitary Star*, 292.
4. Haley, *Sam Houston*, 362.
5. De Bruhl, *Sword of San Jacinto*, 380.
6. Haley, *Sam Houston*, 364.
7. Ibid.
8. Wisehart, *Sam Houston*, 581.
9. Haley, *Sam Houston*, 263.

CHAPTER 19

1. Michael Korda, *Clouds of Glory: The Life and Legend of Robert E. Lee* (New York: Harper, 2014), xvi.
2. De Bruhl, *Sword of San Jacinto*, 383.
3. Roberts, *Star of Destiny*, 285.
4. De Bruhl, *Sword of San Jacinto*, 381.

5. Ibid., 381–82.

6. Woodward, *For Texas and the Union*, 91.

7. Haley, *Sam Houston*, 369.

8. Wisehart, *Sam Houston*, 583.

9. Paula Mitchell Marks, "Maverick, Samuel Augustus," *Handbook of Texas Online*, http://www.tshaonline.org/handbook/online/articles/fma84, uploaded on June 15, 2010, modified on December 7, 2015, published by the Texas State Historical Association.

10. Campbell, *Sam Houston*, 145.

11. Ford, *Rip Ford's Texas*, 204.

12. Jerry Thompson, "Cortina, Juan Nepomuceno," *Handbook of Texas Online*, http://www.tshaonline.org/handbook/online/articles/fco73, uploaded on June 12, 2010, modified on March 28, 2016, published by the Texas State Historical Association.

13. Ford, *Rip Ford's Texas*, 276.

14. De Bruhl, *Sword of San Jacinto*, 382.

15. Ford, *Rip Ford's Texas*, 262.

16. Campbell, *Sam Houston*, 145.

17. Korda, *Clouds of Glory*, 144.

18. Douglas Southall Freeman, *Lee: An Abridgment of* R. E. Lee, *Volumes I–IV* (New York: Touchstone, 1991), 101.

19. Korda, *Clouds of Glory*, 213–14.

20. De Bruhl, *Sword of San Jacinto*, 384.

21. Friend, *Sam Houston*, 303.

22. De Bruhl, *Sword of San Jacinto*, 384.

23. Roberts, *Star of Destiny*, 291.

24. Roberts, *Personal Correspondence*, 4:321.

CHAPTER 20

1. Campbell, *Sam Houston*, 146.

2. Ibid., 147.

3. Braider, *Solitary Star*, 299.

4. Campbell, *Sam Houston*, 148.

5. David Herbert Donald, *Lincoln* (New York: Simon & Schuster, 1995), 243–44.

6. Campbell, *Sam Houston*, 148.

7. Wisehart, *Sam Houston*, 587.

8. Sam Houston, "Letter from Sam Houston Withdrawing from the Canvass," *New York Times*, August 16, 1860.

9. Houston, *Writings*, 8:109.

10. Haley, *Sam Houston*, 369–70.

11. Roberts, *Star of Destiny*, 287.

12. Ibid., 287–88.

13. Williams, *Sam Houston*, 333.
14. Friend, *Sam Houston*, 329.
15. Haley, *Sam Houston*, 371.
16. Roberts, *Star of Destiny*, 293.

CHAPTER 21

1. Seale, *Sam Houston's Wife*, 204.
2. De Bruhl, *Sword of San Jacinto*, 391.
3. Ibid.
4. Campbell, *Sam Houston*, 154.
5. Ibid., 155.
6. James Crutchfield, *It Happened in Texas: Remarkable Events That Shaped Texas History* (New York: Rowman & Littlefield, 1996), 53.
7. Roberts, *Star of Destiny*, 298.
8. Haley, *Sam Houston*, 390.
9. Albert Castel, "Sam Houston's Last Fight," *American Heritage Magazine* 17, no. 1 (1965): 80.
10. Brands, *Lone Star Nation*, 522–23.
11. James, *The Raven*, 410; Ida M. Tarbell, *The Life of Abraham Lincoln* (New York: McClure, Philips, 1900), 2:69–70.
12. Hamilton and Hunt, *My Master*, 76.
13. Haley, *Sam Houston*, 394.

CHAPTER 22

1. Hamilton, *Prologue to Conflict*, 79.
2. Wisehart, *Sam Houston*, 618.
3. Houston, *Writings*, 8:295–300.
4. Haley, *Sam Houston*, 397.
5. Houston, *Writings*, 8:301–5.
6. Ibid., 305–7.
7. Seale, *Sam Houston's Wife*, 215.
8. De Bruhl, *Sword of San Jacinto*, 398.
9. Seale, *Sam Houston's Wife*, 214.
10. Ibid., 213.
11. Ibid., 217.
12. Haley, *Sam Houston*, 402.
13. Seale, *Sam Houston's Wife*, 218.
14. Ibid., 220.
15. Ibid.
16. Friend, *Sam Houston*, 351.
17. James, *The Raven*, 421.

CHAPTER 23

1. Roberts, *Star of Destiny*, 313–18.
2. Roberts, *Star of Destiny*, 313.
3. Seale, *Sam Houston's Wife*, 222.
4. Ibid., 123.
5. De Bruhl, *Sword of San Jacinto*, 399.
6. James, *The Raven*, 424.
7. Walter M. Woodward, *Sam Houston Memorial Museum: Honoring the Life and Times of Sam Houston* (Lawrenceburg, IN: Creative Company, 2013), 18.
8. Ibid.
9. Seale, *Sam Houston's Wife*, 224.
10. Gary Cartwright, *Galveston: A History of the Island* (Fort Worth: Texas Christian University Press, 1991), 106–7.
11. Haley, *Sam Houston*, 408.
12. Seale, *Sam Houston's Wife*, 225.
13. Friend, *Sam Houston*, 339.
14. Haley, *Sam Houston*, 409.
15. Friend, *Sam Houston*, 352.
16. Houston, *Writings*, 8:327–39.
17. Brands, *Lone Star Nation*, 460.
18. Hamilton and Hunt, *My Master*, 93.
19. De Bruhl, *Sword of San Jacinto*, 401.
20. Seale, *Sam Houston's Wife*, 225.
21. Friend, *Sam Houston*, 352.
22. Hamilton, *Sam Houston*, 118.
23. Seale, *Sam Houston's Wife*, 231.
24. Wisehart, *Sam Houston*, 592.
25. De Bruhl, *Sword of San Jacinto*, 402.
26. Roberts, *Star of Destiny*, 323.
27. Hamilton and Hunt, *My Master*, 119.
28. Ibid., 100–101.
29. Roberts, *Star of Destiny*, 320.
30. Hamilton and Hunt, *My Master*, 101.
31. Ibid., 125.
32. Randolph B. Campbell, *An Empire for Slavery: The Peculiar Institution in Texas* (Baton Rouge: Louisiana State University Press, 1989), 207.
33. De Bruhl, *Sword of San Jacinto*, 401.
34. Roberts, *Star of Destiny*, 323.
35. Ibid., 324.
36. Haley, *Sam Houston*, 416; Wisehart, *Sam Houston*, 650.
37. Seale, *Sam Houston's Wife*, 232.
38. Ibid., 233.
39. Ibid., 232.
40. Ibid., 233.

CHAPTER 24

1. Roberts, *Star of Destiny*, 334.
2. Hamilton and Hunt, *My Master*, 124.
3. Prather and Monday, *From Slave to Statesman*, 186.
4. Seale, *Sam Houston's Wife*, 257.
5. Roberts, *Star of Destiny*, 350.

CHAPTER 25

1. George N. Green, "Houston, Andrew Jackson," *Handbook of Texas Online*, http://www.tshaonline.org/handbook/online/articles/fho69, uploaded on June 15, 2010, modified on March 26, 2014, published by the Texas State Historical Association.
2. George N. Green, "O'Daniel, Wilbert Lee (Pappy)," *Handbook of Texas Online*, http://www.tshaonline.org/handbook/online/articles/fod11, uploaded on June 15, 2010, modified on February 22, 2016, published by the Texas State Historical Association.
3. Green, "Houston."
4. Woodward , *Sam Houston Memorial Museum.*

EPILOGUE

1. Ellen Maury Slayden, *Journal of a Washington Wife* (New York: Harper & Row, 1962), 54.
2. Ibid., 310.
3. Dan Rather, Introduction to *From Slave to Statesman: The Legacy of Joshua Houston* (Denton: University of North Texas Press, 1993).
4. Brands, *Lone Star Nation*, 523.

AUTHOR'S NOTES AND ACKNOWLEDGMENTS

1. Alan Axelrod, Introduction to *The Illustrated Edition of Sandburg's* Life of Lincoln (New York: Sterling, 2007), 7.

Bibliography

Aikman, Lonnelle. *We the People: The Story of the United States Capitol*. Washington, DC: US Capitol Historical Society, 1993.

Asimov, Isaac. *Our Federal Union: The United States from 1816 to 1865*. Boston: Houghton Mifflin, 1975.

Axelrod, Alan. Introduction to *The Illustrated Edition of Sandburg's* Life of Lincoln. New York: Sterling, 2007.

Benet, Stephen Vincent. "The Devil and Daniel Webster." In *Selected Works of Stephen Vincent Benet*, vol. 2, *Prose*, 32–46. New York: Farrar & Rinehart, 1942.

Benham, Priscilla Myers. "Rusk, Thomas Jefferson." *Handbook of Texas Online*. http://www.tshaonline.org/handbook/online/articles/fru16. Uploaded on June 15, 2010. Modified on July 18, 2016. Published by the Texas State Historical Association.

Bollaert, William. *William Bollaert's Texas*. Norman: University of Oklahoma Press, 1989.

Braider, Donald. *Solitary Star: A Biography of Sam Houston*. New York: G. P. Putnam's Sons, 1974.

Brands, H. W. *Andrew Jackson: His Life and Times*. New York: Random House / Anchor, 2005.

———. *Lone Star Nation: How a Ragged Army of Volunteers Won the Battle for Texas Independence and Changed America*. New York: Doubleday, 2004.

Brissette, Danielle. "Slavery in the Houston Household." *Sam Houston Memorial Museum Blog*. December 28, 2012. http://samhoustonmemorialmuseum.blogspot.com/2012/12/slavery-in-houston-household.html.

Burstein, Andrew. *The Passions of Andrew Jackson*. New York: Knopf, 2003.

Byrd, Robert C. *The Senate, 1789–1989: Classic Speeches, 1830–1993*. Washington, DC: Government Printing Office, 1994.

Calhoun, John C. "Speech on the Oregon Bill." In *Union and Liberty: The Political Philosophy of John C. Calhoun*, ed. Ross M. Lence. Indianapolis: Liberty Fund, 1992. http://teachingamericanhistory.org/library/document/oregon-bill-speech/.

Campbell, Randolph B. *An Empire for Slavery: The Peculiar Institution in Texas*. Baton Rouge: Louisiana State University Press, 1989.

———. *Gone to Texas: A History of the Lone Star State*. New York: Oxford University Press, 2012.

———. *Sam Houston and the American Southwest*. New York: HarperCollins, 1993.

Cartwright, Gary. *Galveston: A History of the Island*. Fort Worth: Texas Christian University Press, 1991.

Castel, Albert. "Sam Houston's Last Fight." *American Heritage Magazine* 17, no. 1 (1965): 80.

Churchman, Joseph, and James Churchman. The Eagle Map of the United States Engraved for *Rudiments of National Knowledge*. Osher Map Library, Smith Center for Cartographic Education, 1833. http://www.oshermaps.org/exhibitions/map-commentaries/eagle-map.

Connor, Seymour V. "Rankin, Melinda." *Handbook of Texas Online*. http://www.tshaonline.org/handbook/online/articles/fra39. Uploaded on June 15, 2010. Published by the Texas State Historical Association.

Crane, William Carey. *Life and Select Literary Remains of Sam Houston of Texas*. Dallas: W. G. Scarff, 1884.

Crutchfield, James. *It Happened in Texas: Remarkable Events That Shaped Texas History*. New York: Rowman & Littlefield, 1996.

Curtis, Gregory. "Sam Houston." *American History* 47, no. 6 (February 2013): 26–32.

Daniel, Clifton. "1850." In *Chronicle of America*, 338–39. New York: Simon & Schuster, 1989.

De Bruhl, Marshall. *The Sword of San Jacinto: A Life of Sam Houston*. New York: Random House, 1993.

Donald, David Herbert. *Lincoln*. New York: Simon & Schuster, 1995.

Dragonwagen, Crescent. *The Cornbread Gospel*. New York: Workman, 2007.

Dwyer, Charles L., and Gerald L. Holder. "Huntsville, TX." *Handbook of Texas Online*. http://www.tshaonline.org/handbook/online/articles/heh03. Uploaded on June 15, 2010. Published by the Texas State Historical Association.

Estill, Mary S. *Vision Realized: A History of Sam Houston State University*. Huntsville, TX: Sam Houston State University Press, 1970.

Fehrenbach, T. R. *Lone Star: A History of Texas and the Texans*. New York: American Legacy Press, 1983.

Fete, Emerson David. *History of the United States*. New York: Henry Holt, 1916.

Flanagan, Sue. *Sam Houston's Texas*. Austin: University of Texas Press, 1964.

Ford, John Salmon. *Rip Ford's Texas*. Austin: University of Texas Press, 1987.

Freeman, Douglas Southall. *Lee: An Abridgment of* R. E. Lee, *Volumes I–IV*. New York: Simon & Schuster / Touchstone, 1991.

Friend, Llerena. *Sam Houston, the Great Designer*. Austin: University of Texas Press, 1954.

Green, George N. "Houston, Andrew Jackson." *Handbook of Texas Online*. http://www.tshaonline.org/handbook/online/articles/fho69. Uploaded on June 15, 2010. Modified on March 26, 2014. Published by the Texas State Historical Association.

———. "O'Daniel, Wilbert Lee (Pappy)." *Handbook of Texas Online*. http://www.tshaonline.org/handbook/online/articles/fod11. Uploaded on June 15, 2010. Modified on February 22, 2016. Published by the Texas State Historical Association.

Haley, James L. *Sam Houston*. Norman: University of Oklahoma Press, 2002.

Hamilton, Holman. *Prologue to Conflict: The Crisis and Compromise of 1850*. Lexington: University Press of Kentucky, 2005.

Hamilton, Jeff, and Lenoie Hunt. *My Master: the Inside Story of Sam Houston and His Times.* Austin: State House Press, 1992.

Hazlewood, Claudia. "Archive War." *Handbook of Texas Online.* http://www.tshaonline.org/handbook/online/articles/mqa02. Uploaded on June 9, 2010. Modified on August 26, 2016. Published by the Texas State Historical Association.

Henson, Margaret Swett, and Donald E. Willett. *The Texas That Might Have Been: Sam Houston's Foes Write to Albert Sidney Johnston.* College Station: Texas A&M University Press, 2009.

Houston, Sam. "Speech in Opposition to the Kansas-Nebraska Bill, February 15, 1854." In Houston, *Writings*, 5:469–503.

———. "Speech on the Subject of Compromise, Feb. 8, 1850." In Houston, *Writings*, 5:119–44.

———. *Writings of Sam Houston, 1813–1863.* Edited by Amelia W. Williams and Eugene C. Barker. Vols. 1–8. Austin: University of Texas Press, 1943.

Hoyt, Edwin P. *Zachary Taylor.* Chicago: Reilly & Lee, 1966.

Hutchinson, Kay Bailey. *Unflinching Courage: Pioneering Women Who Shaped Texas.* New York: Harper, 2013.

James, Marquis. *The Raven: A Biography of Sam Houston.* 1929. Reprint, Austin: University of Texas Press, 1988.

Kennedy, John F. *Profiles in Courage.* New York: Perennial, 1964.

Korda, Michael. *Clouds of Glory: The Life and Legend of Robert E. Lee.* New York: Harper, 2014.

Lack, Paul D. "Consultation." *Handbook of Texas Online.* http://www.tshaonline.org/handbook/online/articles/mjc08. Uploaded on June 12, 2010. Published by the Texas State Historical Association.

Lehmann, Alan Dean. "Trapped in Texas." Master's thesis, Sam Houston State University, 1995.

Leigh, Fannie Bush. "Recollections." N.d. Sam Houston Memorial Library Manuscript Collection, Huntsville.

Lester, Charles Edward. *The Life of Sam Houston: The Only Authentic Memoir of Him Ever Published.* New York: J. C. Derby, 1855.

Lewis, Walker. *Speak for Yourself, Daniel: A Life of Webster in His Own Words.* New York: Houghton Mifflin, 1969.

Lyman, S. P. *Life and Memorials of Dan. Webster.* Vol. 2. Appleton, MN: Appleton Press, 1855. http://www.ebooksread.com/authors-eng/s-p-samuel-p-lyman/life-and-memorials-of-daniel-webster-volume-2-amy.shtml.

Marks, Paula Mitchell. "Maverick, Samuel Augustus." *Handbook of Texas Online.* http://www.tshaonline.org/handbook/online/articles/fma84. Uploaded on June 15, 2010. Modified on December 7, 2015. Published by the Texas State Historical Association.

Marvell, Andrew. "To His Coy Mistress" (ca. 1650). In *The New Oxford Book of English Verse, 1250–1950*, edited by Helen Gardner, 334–35. New York: Oxford University Press, 1972.

Meacham, Jon. *American Lion: Andrew Jackson in the White House.* New York: Random House, 2009.

Michener, James A. *The Eagle and the Raven.* Austin: State House Press, 1990.

Miller Center of Public Affairs, University of Virginia. "James Buchanan: Foreign Affairs." US Presidents, 2017. https://millercenter.org/president/buchanan/foreign-affairs.

Prather, Patricia, and Jane Monday. *From Slave to Statesman: The Legacy of Joshua Houston.* Denton: University of North Texas Press, 1995.

Rankin, Melinda. *Texas in 1850.* Boston: Damrell & Moore, 1850.

Rather, Dan. Introduction to *From Slave to Statesman: The Legacy of Joshua Houston.* Denton: University of North Texas Press, 1993.

Richardson, Rupert, and Adrian Anderson. *Texas: The Lone Star State.* Englewood Cliffs, NJ: Prentice Hall, 1993.

Roberts, Madge Thornall, ed. *The Personal Correspondence of Sam Houston.* 4 vols. Denton: University of North Texas Press, 1996–2001.

———. *Star of Destiny: The Private Life of Sam and Margaret Houston.* Denton: University of North Texas Press, 2001.

Schmidt, James M. *Galveston and the Civil War: An Island City in the Maelstrom.* Charleston, SC: History Press, 2012.

Seale, William. *Sam Houston's Wife: A Biography of Margaret Lea Houston.* Norman: University of Oklahoma Press, 1970.

Shakespeare, William. *Hamlet, Prince of Denmark.* Folger Shakespeare Library ed. New York: Washington Square Press, 1992.

Sharp, Ed. "Interview." Reprinted in the *New York Times*, November 6, 1892.

Shaw, John. *JFK in the Senate: Pathway to the Presidency.* New York: St. Martin's Press, 2013.

Silverthorne, Elizabeth. *Plantation Life in Texas.* College Station: Texas A&M University Press, 1986.

Slayden, Ellen Maury: *Journal of a Washington Wife.* New York: Harper & Row, 1962.

Smithwick, Noah. *The Evolution of a State: Recollections of Old Texas Days.* Austin: University of Texas Press,1983.

Spain, Charles A., Jr. "Flags of Texas." *Handbook of Texas Online.* http://www.tshaonline.org/handbook/online/articles/msf01. Uploaded on June 12, 2010. Modified on November 28, 2016. Published by the Texas State Historical Association.

Standford, Les. *The Man Who Invented Christmas: How Charles Dickens's* A Christmas Carol *Rescued His Career and Revived Our Holiday Spirits.* New York: Crown, 2008.

Tarbell, Ida M. *The Life of Abraham Lincoln.* Vol. 2. New York: McClure, Philips, 1900.

Tennyson, Alfred Lord. "Ulysses" (1833). In *The Norton Anthology of English Literature: The Major Authors*, 6th ed., edited by M. H. Abrams, 1891–93. New York: W. W. Norton, 1962.

Thompson, Jerry. "Cortina, Juan Nepomuceno." *Handbook of Texas Online.* http://www.tshaonline.org/handbook/online/articles/fco73. Uploaded on June

12, 2010. Modified on March 28, 2016. Published by the Texas State Historical Association.

Tindall, George Brown, and David E. Shi. *America: A Narrative History*. New York: W. W. Norton, 1992.

Walker, Donald R. *A Frontier Texas Mercantile: The History of Gibbs Brothers and Company, Huntsville, 1841–1940*. Huntsville: Texas Review Press, 1997.

———. "Texas State Penitentiary at Huntsville." *Handbook of Texas Online*. http://www.tshaonline.org/handbook/online/articles/jjt01. Uploaded on June 15, 2010. Published by the Texas State Historical Association.

Waugh, John C. *On the Brink of Civil War: The Compromise of 1850 and How It Changed the Course of American History*. New York: Rowman & Littlefield, 2003.

Webster, Daniel. "Speech of the Honorable Daniel Webster, on the Compromise Bill: Delivered in the Senate of the United States, on the 17th Day of July, 1850." HathiTrust Digital Library. https://catalog.hathitrust.org/Record/101715726.

Whittier, John Greenleaf. "Ichabod." In *The Norton Anthology of American Literature*, shorter 4th ed. 637. New York: W. W. Norton, 1979.

Williams, John Hoyt. *Sam Houston: The Life and Times of the Liberator of Texas, an Authentic American Hero*. New York: Simon & Schuster/Touchstone, 1993.

Wisehart, M. K. *Sam Houston: American Giant*. Washington, DC: Robert B. Luce, 1962.

Woodward, Walter M. "Henderson Yoakum, Texas Historian." Master's thesis. Sam Houston State University, 1994.

———. *Sam Houston: For Texas and the Union*. New York: Rosen Publishing Group, 2001.

———. *Sam Houston Memorial Museum: Honoring the Life and Times of Sam Houston*. Lawrenceburg, IN: Creative Company, 2013.

Wylie, Arthur. *The Life and Times of Sam Houston*. Sec. 2, "Ancestry and Youth." 1855. Reprint, Raleigh, NC: LuLu Press, 2014.

Yoakum, Henderson K. *History of Texas: From Its First Settlement in 1685 to Its Annexation to the United States in 1846*. Sam Houston Memorial Museum Collection, Huntsville.

Index